Salt Water Tales

The Strange and Tragic, Illustrated.

The Canada Council | Le Conseil des Arts
for the Arts | du Canada

We acknowledge the support of The Canada Council for the Arts for our
publishing program.

We acknowledge the financial support of the Government of Canada through the Book
Publishing Industry Development Program (BPIDP) for our
publishing program.

∞ Printed on acid-free paper

Published by
CREATIVE PUBLISHERS
an imprint of CREATIVE BOOK PUBLISHING
a Transcontinental Inc. associated company
P.O. Box 8660, St. John's, Newfoundland and Labrador A1B 3T7

First Printing October 2004
Second Printing July 2005
Typeset in Times New Roman

Printed in Canada by:
TRANSCONTINENTAL INC.

National Library of Canada Cataloguing in Publication

Parsons, Robert Charles, 1944-
Salt water tales / Robert C. Parsons ; illustrated by Mel D'Souza.

ISBN 1-894294-79-3

1. Shipwrecks--Newfoundland and Labrador--History.
2. Seafaring life--Newfoundland and Labrador--History. I. Title.

FC2170.S5P3718 2004   971.8
C2004-905675-1

Salt Water Tales

The Strange and Tragic, Illustrated.

Florence:
Great to meet you!
Robert Parsons

July 24 2000

Robert C. Parsons

Illustrated by
Mel D'Souza

Creative
BOOK PUBLISHING
TUCKAMORE BOOKS • KILLICK PRESS • CREATIVE PUBLISHERS

St. John's, Newfoundland
2004

Salt Water Tales

The Strange and Tragic, Illustrated

Dedication:

To Donna Francis (Sales/Marketing) and her Creative Publishers team, Angela Pitcher (General Manager), Joanne Snook-Hann (Cover design) and Gail Hearn (Layout and design artist), who all worked together diligently to make this book possible. Also to Creative Publishers who took a chance on me many years ago and for that I am grateful.

Robert C. Parsons
32 Pearson Place
Grand Bank, NL A0E 1W0
robert.parsons2@nf.sympatico.ca
website: http://shipwrecks.nf.ca
October 2004

"Preserving Newfoundland and Labrador's Maritime History, One Tale at a Time"

Table of Contents

Volume One

Chapter 1
Early and Obscure

Newfoundland has had its share of unsolved mysteries of the sea; many ships left island ports and never returned, some sailing only a short distance across a bay, others relatively longer distances to the seal fishery or to foreign ports across the ocean. *Salt Water Tales: The Strange and Tragic, Illustrated* documents these and as well relates the hardships of mariners whose ships were wrecked on foreign shores or close to home.

One of the earliest calamities with widespread destruction of island ships and lives occurred during a storm that swept Newfoundland on September 11, 1775. Early pioneers remembered and talked of the tremendous loss of shipping and lives although not much as been written of this cataclysmic event, often referred to as "The Year of the Great Storm."

According to records the sea rose suddenly to a height of 30 feet on the east coast, drove 700 small boats ashore, sank eleven and drowned most of their crews. From Harbour Grace to Grates Cove, 300 boats were lost; scores of people perished trying to save property and stages, flakes, fish stores and thousands of quintals of fish were swept away.

Judge Prowse, in his history of Newfoundland, says, "...300 people along Newfoundland's coast lost their lives." For weeks after the Great Storm, dead bodies washed up on the shores and in the fall fishermen frequently discovered bodies in their herring nets.

Another early and equally obscure wreck at Baccalieu Tickle on March 18, 1823. The Cupids schooner *Brothers*, in command of Captain John Bundle, left that town for the ice and the seals, but wrecked on Baccalieu. Twenty-eight men perished out of a crew of 32.

Because some stories have little documented information, there are many brief vignettes in this section of *Salt Water Tales*. My choice was to bring it to you, rather than omit the tale. Where possible here as in other sections I have gone through great lengths to find the names of lost or surviving crewmen from the disasters.

Inspiration to research and write the first story came from a line drawing of the wreck of the *Arctic* supplied by Captain Hubert Hall. The terrible scene presented in the image piqued me to enquire into the date of the tragedy off Newfoundland; thus I located the details.

The question of what happened to Paul Hall and his crew came from an e-mail in the late 1990s from the missing man's descendant, Peggy Bennett of Kippens.

I had looked through all St. John's papers for news of Hall's ship; then finally I went to the Bay of Islands newspaper and found a brief article. Between the two sources a story emerged.

Yet, there were frustrations. For the tale of the *Victory*, despite a long search I could find no list of the crew.

Collision off Cape Race

Date:	*09, 1854*
Location:	*Off Cape Race*
Fatalities:	*370?*
Remarks:	*"Arctic"*
	& "Vesta" Collide

"...and the surface of the sea was strewn with human beings who had jumped or fallen overboard, to whom, however, it was impossible for us to render any assistance and we soon lost sight of all..."

Mr. Baalham, Survivor, Second Officer of the steamer Arctic.

The Collins Line paddle steamer *Arctic* was running in thick fog about 65 miles southeast of Cape Race. The 260 passengers and crew of 175 had thus far enjoyed the trip from Liverpool, England. They were only a day or so away from their destination, New York; though many were never to see the city. Although one of the fastest transatlantic ships of its age, the 284-foot long *Arctic* had two structural problems: it had a wooden hull, most other ships in its class had iron hulls. Also the liner didn't have any watertight compartments in case the wooden hull - which could be easily punctured by an iceberg or another ship - took on water. And furthermore, it had only six hand pumps to remove water.

Captain James Luce had his son with him on the voyage. Also aboard were Mrs. Collins, her daughter and son; Mrs. Collins was the wife of the founder of Collins Line, Edward Collins.

Early Wednesday morning September 27, 1854, Captain Luce had not ordered speed reduced despite the fog and continued running about 12 knots an hour. About noon the French vessel *Vesta* ploughed into the side of *Arctic*. What happened next was described by *Arctic*'s second officer as "chaos and disaster."

Filled with 147 seasonal fishermen returning home and a crew of 50, the merchant screw steamer *Vesta* from St. Pierre to Granville, France, settled lower and lower in the water. *Vesta* was doing about eight knots and, in the impact, its bow was completely shattered and the foremast broke off. One man was killed and others were seriously injured.

It looked as if *Vesta* would be the first to sink and many aboard believed the best chance for safety was the *Arctic*. Those on *Vesta* could barely see the other ship through the fog. Some men jumped overboard to get on board *Arctic*, but soon their cries of distress rang out over the water. *Arctic* was slowly drifting away. One of *Vesta*'s lifeboats got away with about 15 people aboard.

Meanwhile aboard *Arctic*, Captain Luce, chief officer Gourley and second officer Baalham assessed the damage: the iron steamer had made three large holes in the ship about 60 feet abaft the stem. Two holes were below the water line, one of which was five and a half feet into the side of the vessel. It seemed clear *Arctic* would go down and soon.

The wheel was put to the starboard, the engine stopped instantly and *Arctic* backed at full steam until it was free from *Vesta*. This took a couple of minutes, but as they could see *Vesta* just off in the distance in the fog, it appeared to be sinking bow first.

Captain Luce immediately gave orders to start up the six pumps and to clear away *Arctic*'s quarter boats; Gourley left the ship in charge of the starboard lifeboat.

As Baalham lowered the port lifeboat, the captain called out, "Hoist up that boat again, Mr. Baalham and come here to me."

Luce ordered Baalham to go up the hold to see what damage had been done. Baalham quickly studied the holes inflicted by *Vesta* and reported back to Captain Luce that the ship would sink soon.

When Luce heard this, he put the *Arctic* ahead at full speed and they bore away northwest by west toward Cape Race. By this time they lost sight of the chief officer's boat and the other steamer which they supposed had already sunk. Baalham said:

We had not been on our course more than
four or five minutes before we ran over a boat and
crew belonging to the *Vesta*, all of whom perished
with the exception of one, a woman,
who caught hold of a rope
hanging over our bow. (A
subsequent report says
this person was Jassonet
Francois.)

As soon as Luce realized
what had happened, he
ordered *Arctic* stopped, but the
engineer said this was impossible as the lower compart-
ments were full of water. In 30 minutes
all the lower stoking fires went out. By now there
was six feet of water fore and aft. The captain ordered out the
lifeboats.

Utter confusion broke out among the passengers and crew,
but a few saner heads manned the pumps and succeeded in light-
ening the ship forward. They hoped to get at the bow where the
worse leaks seemed to be. Many passengers climbed into the
lifeboats which were still hanging in their davits. Forty-five minutes after the collision Baalham went to the captain to report
water was on a level with the lower deck beams and there was no
hope of saving the ship. "Go to your lifeboat station," Captain
Luce told Baalham, "and lower the boats." Baalham recalled:

> On going to those on the port side, I found them
> completely filled with men and women and no pos-
> sibility of getting near them. I immediately went
> starboard and ordered two crew to lower the guard
> boat. I asked the captain what his intentions were
> and he said, 'The ship's fate will be mine.'
> I then asked him if he would allow his
> young son to go with me, as I intended to take a

Early American luxury liner, The Arctic, of the Collins Line sinking after a collision off
Cape Race in 1854, "by which dreadful calamity nearly 300 persons are supposed to have
perished." Lithograph by N. Currier.
Photo/Lithograph of loss of Arctic. Courtesy Capt. Hubert
Hall, Shipsearch (MARINE)

boat, but he returned to me the answer, 'He should share my fate.'

I then jumped into the boat and was ordered by the captain to cut away the tackle falls, and drop under the stern. I did so, at which time about 20 persons jumped overboard of whom we picked up 17 or 18. We then fell in with another lifeboat which had been lowered from the other side and lightened her of part of its complement. This left 19 in that one and 26 in my boat.

Baalham said the last sight he saw of *Arctic*, its rails were level with the water. Many of the lifeboats capsized in the confusion as the crew had left the ship first. At 4:45 p.m. *Arctic* gave its final nod and sank. The captain's son was killed when the paddlewheel housing fell off the ship; Luce and a few other survivors crawled atop this structure and they were eventually picked up. Three lowered lifeboats disappeared and their whereabouts is still unknown.

Baalham, in his description of the wreck to Newfoundland shipping authorities, said the surface of the sea around the sunken ship was "...strewn with human beings who had jumped or fallen overboard, to whom, however, it was impossible for us to render any assistance."

In the thick fog, they lost sight of the sinking ship and those still left on board or in the water. Baalham took charge of both boats and he figured he was less than 60 miles south southeast of Cape Race. After pulling for 42 hours with nothing but the run of the sea to guide them, the survivors reached Broad Cove, about twelve miles north of Cape Race.

The 45 survivors left to walk to Renews; it was a coastal trail, rugged but well-marked. The group reached Renews Friday, September 29. Baalham finishes his tale of the wreck of *Arctic*:

At Renews I obtained and took charge of a small schooner which was hired by the purser and myself and proceeded immediately in search of the wreck or her boats. We cruised around until yesterday (October 2) in a strong gale of wind from the northeast, but could find no trace of ship or boats.

I sent word to Captain Leitch of the steamer *City of Philadelphia*, acquainting him with the catastrophe, who I am informed, sent off two vessels which he had employed about his own ship. (*City of Philadelphia*, on its maiden voyage, was aground near Cape Race, see Chapter 10 in Volume II).

Mr. Alan Goodridge of Renews, the principal mercantile business in the town, also sent a vessel to the scene on Saturday evening, but it has not yet returned. It is with greatest regret I have to report that no trace of the *Arctic* or her boats could be found. No doubt, however, is left on my mind as to the loss of the steamer *Arctic*.

Over a period of two days passing ships picked up several survivors, among them Captain Luce and Jassonet Francois, who had survived two shipwrecks

Public Ledger
October 3 and 10, 1854.

in the same day. Among the bodies found were Mrs. Collins and her children, Luce's son and about 100 others. Of the 435 who had left England in *Arctic*, about 65 survived.

Amid all the trauma over the lost lives and the ship, the fate of the vessel *Vesta* was nearly forgotten. It limped into St. John's on Saturday, September 30. One man had been killed in the collision, and several others, thinking *Vesta* was sinking, jumped overboard to swim to *Arctic* and were drowned. Two lifeboats were lowered; the first sank with no one in it and the second was immediately boarded by two crew and several passengers. These had refused to listen to Captain Duchesne who had pleaded with them to return on board.

The remaining passengers and crew fervently hoped *Arctic* was out there somewhere in the fog and that it would not desert them. Little did they know of the horror transpiring aboard that steamer.

Fortunately, the watertight bulkhead in *Vesta* had not split or opened and Duchesne saw this as an opportunity to save his ship. He gave orders to lighten his vessel by the head, just as Captain Luce had tried with the *Arctic*. Fish, cargo, luggage were tossed over the side; this raised the bow considerably. The added elevation, coupled with the strength of the forward bulkhead, stopped the heavy inrush of water. The passengers and crew stacked about 150 mattresses and blankets behind the safety partition, over which they threw spare sails. The whole batting was firmly secured by board and planks, tied with cables.

The foremast which had broken off was cut away and this too helped raise the head of the vessel. This whole operation, done under stress and fear of sinking, took two days. *Vesta* then ran under little steam to St. John's; fortunately before the rising of a severe gale which came up the evening they sailed in through the Narrows.

One of Duchesne's first tasks was to call a muster of all crew and passengers - 13 were unaccounted for and had perished while trying to abandon ship. St. John's people who went down to the waterfront to visit the disabled *Vesta* marveled at the piece of superior seamanship and unwavering perseverance that succeeded in bringing the wreck into port. Mr. Toussaint, a Frenchman living in St. John's and with Old World connections, spared no trouble and expense to provide for the comfort of nearly 184 shipwrecked survivors.

According to one source, the total number lost from both ships as a result of the collision was over 370 lives. In its day the loss of *Arctic* was the most infamous example of danger and threat in crossing the Atlantic, eventually overshadowed 58 years later by the 1513 lives lost on *Titanic*.

A Story Obsured by Time, New World Island

Date:	*04, 1877*
Location:	*New World Island*
Fatalities:	*14*
Remarks:	*A Sealing Vessel Capsizes*

One of the earliest sea tragedies out of Notre Dame Bay centres on New World Island. There are few details available today except that the lost ship was a sealing schooner from Herring Neck. It left there on Sunday April 8,1877. On a Thursday, April 19, Captain Bartlett arrived in St. John's in his schooner *Herald* and reported the tragedy. Apparently the Herring Neck vessel was lost in the vicinity of Burnt Island in the Bay of Exploits.

All eighteen aboard hailed from Herring Neck, but the only name given in local papers was Captain Francis Miles. Miles and his crew encountered a strong east northeast gale on Wednesday and Miles thought he could make Green Bay.

It is possible the vessel was driven before the wind and the crew could not control its passage or the captain may not have known the hazards of the

Herring Neck

coast. At any rate, the schooner sailed dangerously close to shoals lying eastward of Burnt Island and capsized in the strong ground sea that broke over the shoals. The sea threw the vessel on its side and it stayed that way with masts in the water.

Some of the men cut away a boat and managed to save some oars. Four men clambered aboard and rowed to safety. Fourteen drowned; only four were spared to tell the details of the sad event.

The papers of the day did not record the crew, but family information passed on says that Captain Miles, William Warren, two men named Smart, Peter Grimes, and another man named Miles also perished. Two brothers, Philip and Francis Miles, survived; the latter was not the captain who drowned. Most of the men lost were married with children.

Ballad of the *Bickley*

Date:	*?, 1847*
Location:	*Off Fogo*
Fatalities:	*70*
Remarks:	*"Bickley" Disappears*

In 1847 the Brigus vessel *Bickley* was lost off Fogo as it sailed en route to the Labrador and the summer fishery. The exact date and circumstances are not clear, but apparently there were seventy people - men, women, and children - aboard this ship, commanded by Captain John Penney, who lived in Brigus North. *Bickley* (sometimes spelled *Bickly*) at sixty-four ton, was built in Brigus in 1805. If the latter date is correct, the vessel was at an advanced age - over forty years old - and that may have been a factor in its loss.

The long and poignant poem "The Ballad of the Brig Bickley" written about this tragedy is signed by RMW who, as research indicates was Reverend Father Richard Mark Walker (1859-1941). He was born in Brigus and later served as parish priest in his home community. Rev. Walker composed the folk ballad around 1900 and it was first produced on broadsheet, a large format page, possibly for retail to raise monies for some charitable occasion.

Many years previous to its fatal plunge, the *Bickley* of Brigus was involved in a dramatic incident at sea. In 1828 the ship was owned by Charles Cozens (Cousens), of Brigus who had a business or traded in St. John's. While in command of Captain Nathan Norman, a 21-year-old man of Brigus, the *Bickley* left Halifax for Harbour Grace around the latter part of December, 1828.

Norman should have reached home in about a week, but it turned to be a much longer voyage - a month, then two months. Meanwhile the people of Brigus were frantic with worry, believing the ship had gone down. When April came, most had given up, thinking that *Bickley* was lost with crew.

Needless to say the feelings of joy and thanksgiving were overwhelming when on the last day of April the battered and storm-tossed *Bickley* pulled into Brigus. The story was told that shortly after leaving Nova Scotia the ship had been caught in a ferocious winter gale and was thrown on its beam ends, or parallel to the water. It that condition it drifted for quite awhile with the crew trying their best to right the ship. They succeeded, only to have it happen again and again in the severe January-February storms.

Off the east coast in winter ships are subject to "icing up" when the decks and rigging become coated with frozen spray. As well, the crew had to navigate carefully through ice pans and bergs. Food supplies and water aboard *Bickley* ran out, so that when it finally reached Brigus, the crew was reduced to one pint of water per day for each man.

It's likely *Bickley* harboured in a foreign port for repairs and that caused excessive delay; yet the exact story of the long and torturous voyage is not fully fleshed out. At any rate it survived one epic experience only to go down at sea in 1847, taking many lives with it - some surnames of those aboard *Bickley* are known today: Whelan, Roberts, Finn, Penney, Quinlan, Chancey. Among the victims was the captain's wife, Caroline (Williams) Penney.

The Ballad of the Bickley, Lost 1847

Listen to a tale of woe,
Of more than fifty years ago.

Men of Brigus in the hollow,
If my story you will follow,
You will see the ocean swallow
  Gallant ship and crew.
Fathers brave and braver brothers,
Husbands, sisters, wives and mothers,
Whom the sea in anger smothers,
  And conceals from view.

Three and fifty years I think 'tis,
If old folklore does not trick us,
A staunch vessel sailed from Brigus,
  Bearing friends ye knew.
Stalwart men the loose sheets trimming,
Children rosy-cheeked and women,
Whose bright eyes and tears are dimming
  As they bid adieu.

Sailed the good ship - Penney, master,
Ship that ne-er yet met disaster,
Than she none ere built sailed faster,
  Bearing human freight.
Onward toward their destination,
There to pursue their avocation,
At some far-off fishing station
  Past yon ice-swept Strait.

Down the Bay Conception sailing,
White-capped billows hissing, hailing,
Ne'er once in her true course failing,
  Went the gallant ship.
North towards the Labrador-land,
Which for you men, is bright ore-land,
But for many a No-more-land,
  And last ocean trip.

Fishing season saw them ended,
Sail to boom, and yard saw bended,
Song and laughter heard they blended,
  Brave lads 'fore the mast.
Sound of chain and block prevailing,

Nor good ship nor human ailing,
As they now go onward sailing,
  But their die is cast.

Anxious eyes at home are watching,
Anxious ears with eyes are matching,
Faintest good news gladly catching,
  While fond spirits yearned.
So for days and weeks ensuing,
Phantom ship hearts kept pursuing,
Till at last came bitter rueing -
  She never returned.

There where seagulls loud are screaming,
And the Northern Lights are gleaming,
Ah! Heaven beheld - no idle dreaming,
  Or vain story glossed -
Whelans, Robertses, Finns, with Penney,
Quinlans, Chancey, others many, Seventy
Odd, all told, if any -
  Aye, and all hands - Lost!

There, somewhere in Ocean's keeping,
With the cold wave o'er them sweeping,
They today are rocked - are sleeping,
  Their last sleep, I wot;
While Brigus still doth ask, doth wonder,
How Penney with his crew went under
But thro' storm or leak or blunder,
  Ocean answers not.

L'ENVOI -
'Tis many a day since they sailed away
From the old familiar spot,
Still the Rachel-cry ascends on high
  Because HER sons are not;
'Tis many a day since they sailed away
From home and hearts that yearned, But
Still today do fond ones pray for the
Friends who never returned.

    R.M.W.

One person who researched and commented briefly on Walker's ballad suggested the composition was of considerable poetic merit and that "from the rhyme scheme and the rhythm it could be sung to the tune of the famous Welsh war song *Men of Harlech*."

Captain Bob Bartlett too wrote of the strange disappearance of *Bickley* in his autobiography *The Log of Captain Bob Bartlett*. He says, "Take the case of brigantine *Bickley*, Captain John Penney. It met a howling gale down near Green Bay... It never came back; not a trace of it was ever found. Ninety-seven souls were aboard." According to Bartlett, the night it went down three different families of crew saw tokens or spirits of drowning seamen aboard *Bickley*:

> In one case the mother of one of the boys was sitting darning a sock by her lamp. She was rocking in her chair thinking how happy she would be the next week when her lad came back. Suddenly the door clicked. In walked her only son with soaking clothes and his boots squeaking with water. He stood there swaying before her as if terribly exhausted. But before she could speak he disappeared.
> Pat Clancy (Chancey?) was in the same crew. His wife lived at Cape Ann. She was just getting supper when in walked Pat, the water running off him. He didn't say a word. He just staggered over to the cradle where two baby boys lay and looked down on them. Sadly he shook his head. Then he faded away.

Fourteen years after *Bickley*'s disappearance another obscure tragedy claimed several Conception Bay lives. In 1861 the brig *Hibernia* left Labrador for Harbour Grace. Aboard were Captain James Stapleton and thirty-nine other people en route home from the summer/fall fishery. On October 14, while off Seldom, one of the frequented stops on the three to four day voyage, *Hibernia* sank and all were lost. Again as with *Bickley* the passage of time has obscured details on what caused the end of the ship or exactly who was lost.

Plea for a Light At Cape St. Francis

Date:	*05, 1871*
Location:	*Off Cape St. Francis*
Fatalities:	*23*
Remarks:	*Disappearance of "Dove"*

"Petitions, year after year have been presented to the Newfoundland Assembly for the erection of a Light House at Cape St. Francis. But the government of the day turned a deaf ear to them all."

Thus was the editorial in newspaper *The Patriot* in June 1871. It went on to beg people, someone, anyone to take up the cause "for the recent sad calamities" and hopefully those tragedies "will have the desired effect in bringing government officials to their senses."

One of the earliest recorded disasters off Cape St. Francis happened in early May1840. The 284-ton bark *Atlantic* from Scotland to Quebec ran aground near the Cape. It was loaded with general cargo and had 27 passengers plus the crew. According to the newspapers of the day, "they had a miraculous escape but all succeeded in getting ashore" with the exception of a boy named Hogg who drowned. The survivors came overland into St. John's in a destitute condition and had to appeal to the charitable public for extra clothes.

On May 20, the body of the boy Hogg drifted ashore at Holyrood and was buried there.

Now in May 1871 the papers referred to another disaster. On May 20th Eleazar March left St. John's in his schooner *Dove*, heading for his home in Old Perlican, Trinity Bay. On a Saturday it took on a load of merchandise and general supplies at Baine Johnston and Company Wharf. In addition to Skipper March, aboard *Dove* were 22 people, including two females. Many of the men were sealers who had been to the seal fishery in the spring,

Biscayan Rocks looking from Cape St. Francis

gone to St. John's to buy winter supplies and now were returning to their Trinity Bay homes. Most had cash or their various purchases bought from the proceeds of the spring's work.

The next news of the vessel came Sunday when portions of the wreck and its cargo were seen floating in the neighborhood of Cape St. Francis. No one knew if it had struck an iceberg or ran upon the Brandies Rocks, and what happened would remain a mystery as all had perished.

The identity of those lost was supplied by Rev. Charles Ladner, the Wesleyan preacher at Old Perlican. He also knew that 44 children were left without a breadwinner.

According to *The Patroit* the appalling loss of life was not the only instance of a disaster which had occurred in that dangerous locality:

Several other [disasters] have successively taken place there and many lives have been lost. It was there Captain Calihan and his entire crew went down and periodically the same tale has been related for years back.

Petitions year after year have been presented to the House of Assembly, all hitherto have been abortive...

One of those who had objected against establishing a light at the cape was the Inspector of Lighthouses, Robert Oak. He reasoned that there were too many shoals and rocks outside the cape. Thus a vessel keeping north of any proposed light might still meet disaster upon other shoals. Any light said Oak,should be placed one of the various rocks or islets off the cape - the Biscayan Rocks, or the Brandies shoal, lying less than a mile off shore.

Others reasoned that a fog whistle should be installed at Cape St. Francis. This would be more suitable in foggy weather when a light might not been seen.

Old Perlican People Lost on Dove, May 20, 1871	
Lost	**Dependants**
James Barrett	wife, 2 children
James Barrett (of John)	wife, 6 children
John Barrett	wife, 3 children
Joshua Barrett	wife
Nathan Barrett	wife
Nehemiah Barrett	wife
Mary Ann Burt (Eleazer March's sister)	husband, 8 children
Joseph Button	wife, 4 children
George Chirley	wife, 6 children
William Cox	wife, 5 children
Cecilia Cox	daughter of William
William Day	wife, 2 children
his son John Day	wife, 3 children
his son Simon Day	wife, 1 child
William Froud(e)	wife, 3 children
Eleazar March	wife, 4 children
James March	wife, 3 children
James March (of Andrew)	single
John Reid	single
Eli Strong	wife, 2 children
George Strong	single

No Message from the Missing

Date: 03, 1901
Location: West Coast
Fatalities: 15
Remarks: Disappearance
               of Two Crews

In the spring of 1901 and again in the spring of 1903, two ships both involved in the spring seal fishery, disappeared from Newfoundland's south west coast. Around the turn of the twentieth century, it was the practise for ships from the southwestern corner, (as indeed all the north and west coasts of Newfoundland) to follow the seal herd as they whelped or gave birth on the ice. By March-April the great pans of Arctic ice had drifted down the Strait of Belle Isle and the Gulf of St. Lawrence far enough to make the hunt for seal pelts relatively easy and profitable.

The spring ritual and hunt also had its dangers as men who go "to the ice" will sometimes admit: treacherous seas, unpredictable storms, jagged pans of ice awaiting the unwary ship. Around the turn of the twentieth century the joy and extra cash associated with the seal hunt was overshadowed with gloom and distressing circumstances for families of Codroy and Grand River. For one, the *United Brothers* from Grand River, the story is documented in written accounts and its eventual fate is easier to trace.

UNITED BROTHERS PROVISIONS
1 barrel of pork
1 barrel of beef
1 bag of bread
1/2 barrel flour
a fair supply of tea

The second vessel, which has family tradition sources as well as written accounts, was from Grand River. The calamity is well-known in family circles and is often referred to as "The Tragic Tale of Paul Hall."

In those early years of the seal hunt the settlement of Grand River prepared to outfit its ships for the annual spring event.

Housewives got together what was then called "a bag and barrel" - the supply of clothes, gear and food for the men. These provisions would last several weeks until the loved ones returned home.

One of the most able schooners of Grand River was Captain John Blanchard's 39-ton *United Brothers*. It was built in 1890 by Magloire Blanchard and his son John. Magloire skippered the vessel for years and eventually gave it to his son. The Blanchard family were of French descent and had once lived at Searston.

> **Crew of *United Brothers*, Missing Since March 1901**
>
> John Blanchard, married, Grand River
> Edward Blanchard, single, John's son, Grand River
> Daniel McIsaac, single, a nephew of the Blanchards, Grand River
> John O'Quinn, (Aucoin) single, Grand River
> Nelson Gallop, single, Codroy

In the fall of 1900 Blanchard moored his schooner at Channel to avoid the risk of being frozen in at Grand River, so when spring arrived he was ready. Grand River was a difficult place to enter in the best of times, but during the winter ice conditions and rafting ice, it was near impossible.

To prepare for the fishery, Blanchard left Channel for Grand River on Monday, March 11, 1901, and arrived at "the Gut" the same day. He couldn't get in the harbour for the strong river current and anchored off shore. By early Tuesday morning he ran in and moored within sight of his own house.

But Tuesday opened with bad news. A hurricane, powerful out the east southeast, lashed the sea to a seething foam. It put a great strain on *United Brothers* anchors and at daylight either the chain burst or the anchor dragged and the schooner was driven off to sea. There was nothing any captain could do under such circumstances except run to sea, under "bare poles" with no sail up and wait until the storm was over.

Landsmen peered out to the horizon, but could barely see the schooner with the foam and spray whipped up by the wind. Judging by the direction to which it was headed, wives and friends figured Blanchard was going toward offshore slob ice. A few days previously the same ice, with small bergs and growlers (pans of ice) had been closer to land.

They knew the ship had not yet gotten its full provisions necessary for the month-long duration of the seal hunt. And *United Brothers* was light for it had only a few ton of ballast aboard. Yet another factor weighed on the minds of loved ones; when the schooner was last seen off Grand River, it was coated with ice built up by freezing spray. This would make any schooner unstable and unmanageable in heavy weather.

Within the next several days other ships docked at Channel, Codroy, Grand River, and Port aux Basques but none had any knowledge of *United Brothers*: Captain Carter of the schooner *Jubilee*, Captain Dicks of *Maggie A* had seen nothing. The captain's father, M. Blanchard, believed his son's ship ran for the ice and, in the north wind that persisted, was frozen in. If it didn't show up with the next favourable wind, he held little hope that they would ever be heard from again.

His ominous prediction proved correct in the weeks, months that followed. Eventually *United Brothers* was posted "Missing with Crew" and the mystery remains of how a ship so close to land and home port could vanish forever.

There are connections in time between the spring of 1901 and 1903 and with the uncertain whims of the ocean. On April 17, 1901, George Gallop of Codroy, drowned from the schooner *Minnie F*, captained by Paul Hall, Junior, of Codroy. George Gallop was a relative of Nelson Gallop who was last seen adrift in *United Brothers*.

It is known too that Captain Paul Hall, his crew and ship disappeared "at the ice", but this mystery of the sea is not as well fleshed out as the tale of *United Brothers*. The newspaper *Western Star*, published in Bay of Islands located north of Grand River and Codroy, has a brief item in its March 26, 1902, edition: "Captain Hall sailed for the seal fishery Monday (March 24)."

Family anecdotal information, church records, and ships' registries relate a similar litany of tragedy. The next spring on April 1, 1903, Captain Hall and nine seamen from Codroy and Grand River disappeared after they left for the seal fishery in the

Gulf of St. Lawrence. They were Captain Paul Hall, age 70 and born in Codroy Valley; his son, Paul Joseph Hall, age 28; John Hall, 46; Joseph Barter, 34; Michael Cashin, 21; Thomas Young, 36, William Patten, 24, William Robinson, John Young and John Gallop.

Their vessel was the 33-ton *New Dominion*, once owned by Emanuel Pike of Port aux Basques. Pike had purchased the

thirteen-year-old schooner the year previously at Chezzetcook River in Nova Scotia. Then Paul Hall bought it, but had not insured *New Dominion*. Joe Bruce, an old seadog in the Codroy area, looked at the schooner and voiced the opinion that it was too unseaworthy to put on the water. "Rotten as a peach," he said.

In an instant on the sea, three of the Hall family were lost. The Gallop family too was again faced with tragedy for with the death of John Gallop, that made three Gallop breadwinners who had perished in three years - George on the *Minnie F*, Nelson on *United Brothers* and now John, one of the crew of *New Dominion*.

On June 24, 1903, under *The Western Star*'s heading **Given Up As Lost** reported:

"Friends and relatives of the crew have given up hope of ever seeing their loved ones on *New Dominion* again. Six were married and four men were single. Steamers and vessels have eagerly

sought for some trace of the crew, but all arrive back with no message from the missing."

Victory of Harbour Grace

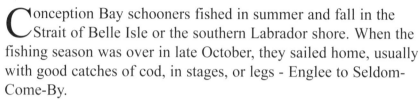

Date:	*12, 1895*
Location:	*Between Labrador & Harbour Grace*
Fatalities:	*15-10?*
Remarks:	*Vessel "Victory" Disappears*

Conception Bay schooners fished in summer and fall in the Strait of Belle Isle or the southern Labrador shore. When the fishing season was over in late October, they sailed home, usually with good catches of cod, in stages, or legs - Englee to Seldom-Come-By.

By the middle of December 1895, all hope of ever hearing any good news of the schooner *Victory* was fading. Captain Robert Bradbury and his crew, all of Harbour Grace, had been missing for over five weeks. News was slow coming at first, but gradually other vessels reported bits and pieces of information which, when totalled, pointed to the loss of the schooner. As a final word on the tragedy the local paper said, "The family and friends of those who have swallowed up by the sea can now but mourn their sudden taking away."

Apparently W. Noel in the schooner *Active* left Englee on October 31 side by side with *Victory*. *Active*, a better sailer, soon outdistanced the other schooner and, on the second evening out from Englee, anchored in Seldom-Come-By. *Active* carried three double-reefed sails up to the time it arrived at Seldom. Noel reasoned that, since there was no wind or sea sufficient to cause anxiety at the time, *Victory* kept on its course, by-passed Seldom, and on the second night out was lost. By that time it must have been in the vicinity of Cabot Island on Newfoundland's Straight Shore. But exactly how and where it met its final fate was a mystery.

Two weeks later, more opinions surfaced. Patrick Keefe, who came to Harbour Grace by the *Flora* brought other details. *Flora* was a schooner commanded by Captain Morrissey, but owned by J.J. Hennessy. Keefe claimed that in the night of October 31 *Flora* passed a schooner in Stag Harbour Run, just off Stag Point.

Captain Morrissey hailed this schooner, but the name could not be heard by anyone on *Flora*. However, in answer to a question of the captain's name, the reply came back, clear and distinct, "Bradbury of Harbour Grace." Morrissey asked Keefe if he knew Bradbury and Keefe said he knew him well. Bradbury also said he departed Englee the previous night and that all the other schooners had left there.

The description of *Victory* agreed with Keefe's knowledge of what he had seen in the night, which was a clear night - no wind, no seas. *Flora* put into New Harbour, Bonavista Bay, (today's Newport) and arrived safely in Harbour Grace on November 3. Keefe concluded that in determining the whereabouts of *Victory*, it would have reached well along Cape Freels before any heavy weather came on that could endanger the schooner.

To add confusion, a story came back to Harbour Grace via the St. John's newspaper *Evening Herald* that wreckage supposedly belonging to *Victory* had been located at Horse Islands off White Bay. Veteran seaman believed this could not be correct. The missing schooner had passed these islands and there was no way possible for such debris to drift from Stag Harbour Run to the Horse Islands.

By the end of the year, Harbour Grace people knew Robert Bradbury and his schooner *Victory* would never be seen again. In the various reports and articles on the schooner's disappearance, the names of other members of the crew were not given.

A Survivor's Tale

Date: *03, 1887*
Location: *Off Fermeuse*
Fatalities: *5*
Remarks: *"Susan" Strikes an Iceberg*

In James Murphy's book *Newfoundland Heroes of the Sea* (1923) there is a sentence which says that Captain Joy of the Carbonear ship *Muriel* rescued three men from the ill-fated *Susan* of St. John's in 1887. This brief and obscure tidbit hints at disaster and heroism. If that's all we had of the event, it would be precious little indeed. But the full extent of the shipwreck comes from the tale of John Lahey, one of *Susan*'s survivors.

"We left St. John's on Friday morning, March 25, " Lahey says, "bound for the West Indies. We got outside all right and a few miles off sailed into the ice which was pretty heavy."

Barquentine *Susan*, chartered by Harvey and Company and loaded with fish, carried eight crew - Captain Michael Ryan, mate John Gaul, cook John Anning, bosun Walter Walsh, seamen Frank Dillon, Thomas Millard, John R. Bailey and Lahey. Lahey belonged to Logy Bay; most of the others lived in St. John's or vicinity.

At any rate, the ice forced Captain Ryan to sail near land, beating in and out all night and the next morning, until the ship was off Fermeuse. It was Saturday, one p.m. Another ship, the Carbonear-owned *Muriel* which had left St. John's a little behind *Susan*, was in the general vicinity off Fermeuse and was also battling the ice. *Muriel* was a three-masted vessel owned by John Rorke.

Photo of *Muriel* (Rorke), above, The Carbonear Vessel that rescued the crew of the *Susan* on March 25, 1887. Courtesy Maritime History Archive, MUN, St. John's

A little after one p.m. the trouble started, as Lahey recalled:

There was a large iceberg on our lee bow, and as the ship near the berg - fearing we could not weather (sail around) it - the captain ordered the helm hard up. But the ship had on too much canvas. The captain called to lower the mainsail and spanker.

All hands were now on deck. About five minutes after *Susan* crashed into the ice and its bows were stove in, the bowsprit and head gear were carried away. The order came to get out the boats.

We let the main topmast staysail down, took the halyards off, hooked them into the jolly boat and launched that all right. Captain Ryan gave orders to get the long boat out; some crew by now were in the jolly boat. The captain, bosun and myself were trying to launch the long boat and managed to get it on the rail, but the mainsail being in the way we could not get it off.

Susan then hove out, or rolled on its beam end.

"She's going now," shouted Captain Ryan. "All hands look after themselves."

The captain and bosun ran for the boats, but were too late. I ran for the weather side of the ship and got the mate up with me. The mate was looking after himself. I did not see him again.

Lost on *Susan*, March 26, 1887

Capt. Michael Ryan of St. John's,
        leaving a wife and 4 children
mate John Gaul, St. John's,
        a wife, no children
Frank Dillon, single, St. John's
John Anning, (or Allen), foreign sailor,
        leaving a family living in St. John's
cook Thomas Millard, single, foreign sailor

All this time - over a half hour - *Susan* was rapidly settling. Five minutes later it sank, but the long boat which had been left on the deck, floated up. Three men - Lahey, Walter Walsh and John Bailey - jumped into it. Lahey heard the captain shout,

"Save me! Save me for the sake of my wife and children!"

Lahey and the others made their way to the captain through dangerous obstacles, rigging, sail, loose lines and ropes threatening to ensnare them and pull all down with it. He recalled:

Evening Mercury headlines
March 28, 1887

We went to his assistance and caught him by the collar of the coat but could not make him let go of the rigging for some time. At last we got him into the boat. While we were hauling the long boat out between the main and mizzen masts the vessel lurched somewhat upright and the jump stay struck the boat, capsizing it.

All hands were now in the water. When I last saw the captain he was holding on to a cork fender. I clung to the long boat's chock (or wooden wedge). Walter Walsh clung to a ladder and two oars. Bailey went under and, coming up, saw the jolly boat a short distance off. Dillon and Millard were in it.

Bailey swam to the boat and got in, but it was nearly full of water, having turned over and then uprighted.

Millard said, "I am frozen."

Millard then fell back; the boat again turned over. By this time Millard and Dillon, who had been into and out of

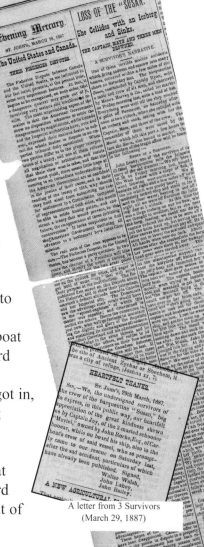

A letter from 3 Survivors
(March 29, 1887)

the water, were exhausted and had lost all strength to fight the battle. Both sank to rise no more.

Bailey had also fallen in the water, but managed to grab the stern of the jolly boat. He clung to it, exhausted.

At this time *Muriel*, which was in the general vicinity also fighting the ice floes, could be seen to back her yards and then lower a boat. Only three of *Susan*'s crew were in sight: Lahey, clinging to the chock of a lifeboat; Bailey, holding on to the stern of the jolly boat, and Walter Walsh. He was holding some debris from the sunken barquentine. It had gone under about three quarters of an hour after it first struck the iceberg.

Captain Joy soon had them aboard the *Muriel*. The three survivors were taken to Freshwater Bay near Fermeuse and on Sunday, March 27, transferred to the S.S. *Hercules* and brought to St. John's.

John Lahey, in his tale to the *Evening Mercury*, couldn't say enough to praise Captain Joy and the crew of *Muriel*. Joy was prompt in launching a lifeboat for had he delayed another few minutes the three survivors would have perished. Once aboard *Muriel* he treated them with every kindness and made them as comfortable as possible. On March 29, Lahey and the others wrote a letter thanking Captain Joy and his crew.

In an ironic twist of fate, a few years after their timely rescue the schooner *Muriel*, Captain Joy and his entire crew were lost while sailing from Europe to Newfoundland.

Chapter 2
Island and Crag

Tales of sailors and ship passengers, men, women and children suddenly thrust ashore upon an island are common in the litany of sea disasters. Money and material possessions meant little if a crag or islet was barren and desolate. Often survival time could be measured in hours rather than days. If the island was larger and had vegetation or human habitation, shelter still had to found quickly, especially in adverse weather conditions.

One of the most frequently told tales of castaways upon a rocky crag is that of the *Queen of Swansea* wrecked on Cape John Gull Island, Notre Dame Bay, on December 11, 1867. During a storm it stranded on the island and the eight crew, six passengers and a local pilot nearly lost their lives right there and then. But eleven people, including two women, reached the barren island, while four were swept away with the wrecked ship and perished. In the long, cold, hungry days that followed, one by one each died on the islet, although in the end some resorted to cannibalism. One of the last to die was Dr. Dowsley of St. John's who kept a detailed diary of the terrible events. The bodies were later discovered by some men from Leading Tickles.

I have never seen (and perhaps one has never been done) an accurate count of the islands around Newfoundland and Labrador; no doubt an undertaking equal to Abraham's task of counting the grains of sand on a seashore. Representing only a mere fraction of stories that could be told about survivors stranded upon islands, *Salt Water Tales* contains nine true accounts of rocks, crags, islets, surrounded by water and the hardships castaways encountered upon them.

One of the stories within this chapter has been published before. "Grim Discovery off Island Harbour, Fogo Island" was presented in my on-line column Tides, Tears and Tales located at www.shipwrecks.nf.ca. I figured most people may not have read it there; thus it also appears in *Salt Water Tales*.

Grim Discovery at Island Harbour

Date:	*09, 1887*
Location:	*Island Harbour*
Fatalities:	*5*
Remarks:	*A Ship and Crew Disappear near Fogo*

It was a tragic sea story, the whole of which is now lost in the pages of time. Descriptions, words, indeed whole paragraphs are missing and only fragments of a story remain. Yet the tale has a beginning and an ending; it's the middle - why a ship drifted ashore and how a crew fought to survive - that is missing.

The first clue to the unraveling of a mystery began on Tuesday, September 27, 1887. It was one of those days sea bird hunters love to be on the water and around the bird rocks. There was not a breath of wind and the water was as smooth as a mill pond. Jacob Ford and John Fooks of Island Harbor, a village on the south end of Fogo Island, were hunting in the tickle or channel between Indian Island and Fogo Island. Ford shot a bird near the Gun Rock and rowed over to pick it up. He noted grease or an oily film floating on the water and, out of curiosity, peered down at the sea bottom. To his surprise and shock he saw, in relatively shallow water, the body of a man lying face down among a quantity of split cod fish strewn on the bottom.

Ford and Fooks immediately proceeded home and organized a search party. There was no time to lose for the fall winds could roil the waters and really hinder search and recovery efforts. By the next morning he, his hunting partner Fooks, William Foley, Martin Foley, James Brown and Samuel Ford went to Gun Rock in a trap skiff. After a diligent drag and search of the bottom in the area they recovered three partially decomposed bodies - males, two were middle-aged. The remains were reverently brought to Fogo, the largest town on the island, where the local magistrate resided. He would make official procedures for identification and arrange a proper and Christian burial, regardless of who the dead men were.

By Thursday, Island Harbour and the whole of Fogo Island were abuzz with speculation and rumor. No one really knew the identity of the drowned men, or what had happened to cause death in the narrow passage between Indian Island and Fogo. It was generally agreed the three victims had been part of the crew of a schooner that dragged its anchors at south end of Change Island on Sunday, September 18. Change Island, also near Fogo, was a much-frequented stopover for fishing ships coming from the Labrador in the fall.

Only debris and wreckage of a vessel could be found at the site. No one knew if the crew had made it ashore, if some had drifted away in small boats, or if all had perished.

Now, with the discovery of bodies, evidence certainly pointed to a sea disaster with no survivors. Fogo's magistrate asked the Methodist clergy, Reverend Jeremiah Embree, to attend the examination of the remains. The magistrate asked Embree to record any identifying marks and to ascertain, if possible, the religious denomination of the deceased. A Mr. Stone, in the absence of the Church of England Rector, also attended the investigation. Within a day, it was agreed between the Magistrate, Rev. Embree and Stone the bodies should be interred in the Methodist Cemetery.

It was noted that one victim had the name "George A. Chalk" tattooed on his left arm and his pocket contained a boat's compass. Another body, that of a younger man, had the initials "J.M." on the left arm.

As evidenced by the name, Chalk, and local knowledge of which ships had stopped in the general area, Fogo Islanders believed the men belonged to Bird Island Cove, located a few miles southeast of Bonavista. Ships from there and the northeast coast of Newfoundland, which includes the towns on the Bonavista Peninsula, regularly engaged in the Labrador fishery. The voyage was relatively long and one of the overnight stops between Bonavista and the Labrador was Change Island.

In time family and loved ones at Bird Island Cove received the news of the shipping disaster. They were grateful some bodies had been recovered and were properly interred. In appreciation for the kind deeds, relatives wrote a thank-you letter to the Fogo Island people.

They knew five men were not coming home - the entire crew of the fishing boat *Brothers*. All had been lost with their ship near Change Island on 18 September: John Chalk, age 47, who left a wife and a large family; William Coles, 32, wife and 3 children as well as aged parents; Artellius Chalk, 27, wife and one child; George Chalk, 25, and John Martin, 20. Artellius and George were sons of Elias Chaulk; John was Elias' brother — all were from the North Side of Bird Island Cove.

Today Bird Island Cove is called Elliston and the surname Chalk generally spells Chaulk.

As a sub-note on "Grim Discovery at Island Harbour": the story evolved as I searched for information on the loss of a ship *Brothers*. I found two pieces of information: *The Evening Mercury* October 24, 1887, and in the October 26, 1887, edition of *The Evening Telegram* I located a letter sent by an anonymous writer in Bird Island Cove. It was headed **Our Bereaved Fisher Folk: Concerning the Bird Island Cove Disaster**. The article thanked the people of Island Harbour and described the memorial service for the lost men. I also received confirmation and other details of the Chaulk and Cole men from Thomas Cole via e-mail. One family name in this story is of interest - Fooks. I thought this was a mistake in the original story, for no such surname exists in Newfoundland today. But the Fooks family and a merchant once resided in nearby Boyd's Cove, and the name on a local headstone verifies this.

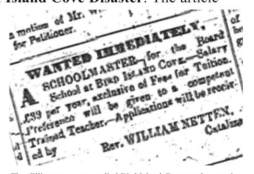

That Elliston was once called Bird Island Cove can be seen in this advertisement for a teacher in the September 23, 1870, newspaper. The annual salary at £39 would be about $94 in today's currency.

Stranded on Scaterie

Date: 11, 1927
Location: Scaterie
Fatalities: none
Remarks: Stranded on Scaterie Island

In the fall of 1927 a St. John's schooner met its end on Nova Scotian shores. Although there was no loss of life when *Admiral Drake* stranded on Scaterie Island, located on the eastern tip of Cape Breton, it became a matter of how and when the crew would get off the island. For four days wind and heavy seas prevented the castaways from reaching mainland Nova Scotia. When weather abated they finally left the island, traveled to Sydney and from there made their way to Newfoundland.

On November 26, the tern schooner *Admiral Drake* grounded on the shores of Scaterie. At eight thirty p.m. while en route to Sydney from St. John's it struck Eastern Rock, filled with water and broke apart. Captain Arnold Benson, mate Leonard Dale, bosun Armand Segullian, cook William Pike, seamen Michael Lenham, Albert Parsons, William Kerrivan and Raymond Murray, all of St. John's or Carbonear area reached shore in their own boats.

Built in Shelburne in 1916 *Admiral Drake*, netting three hundred nine ton, was the largest tern schooner launched by builder G.A. Cox up to that year. It measured 130 feet long and thirty-two feet wide. Owner A.S. Rendell and

CREW ADMIRAL DRAKE ARE STILL MAROONED

Ship was Driven on Scatarie by Storm While on Way From Sydney to St. John's

Halifax, Nov. 23.—(C. P.)—The crew of the St. John's schooner Admiral Drake are still marooned on Scaterie Island off the Cape Breton coast, where the ship was driven after a buffeting gale on Saturday afternoon, while on a voyage to Sydney in ballast from St. John's. The ship became a total loss, but ...

E DAILY NEWS

ST. JOHN'S, NEWFOUNDLAND, MONDAY, NOVEMBER 28, 1927.   Price Two Cents   No. 270.

OF ST. JOHN'S TOTAL WRECK ON SCATARIE ISLAND

The Daily News of November 28, 1927

SCHR. ADMIRAL DRAKE WRECKED ON SCATERIE

Into Nfld. Vessel Total Loss—Crew Rescued but Still on Island

Halifax, Nov. 27—(C.P.)—Advices from Scaterie Island to-day stated that the schooner Admiral Drake,

Company of St. John's placed their vessel in the general trade between Newfoundland and Nova Scotia. At the time of its loss, *Admiral Drake* carried no cargo, but ballast.

The lighthouse on Scaterie.

Four or five days later the Italian steamer *Generale Demitti* sighted part of *Drake*'s hull off Flint Island, about three miles from Scaterie. On December 1, the captain of S.S. *Haugerland* informed Vincent Mullins of the Marine and Fisheries Department at Sydney the wrecked schooner had split from end to end and floated in two sections off Flint Island. Government cutter *Margaret* was sent to remove the wreckage, a menace to navigation

The Bull, Cow and Calf

Date: *08, 1843*
Location: *Calf Rock*
Fatalities: *1*
Remarks: *Wreck of "Customer"*

In 1827 the people of Lamaline had plenty to complain about and they expressed their discontent in a letter to the Newfoundland government. "Every day," they said, "we are exposed to fresh insults and have suffered long enough." They put in writing their annoyance, citing examples of damage caused by the French. The French fleet, out of France and using St. Pierre as a base, illegally fished the prolific cod grounds just off Lamaline and hurled insults and verbal abuse at the people.

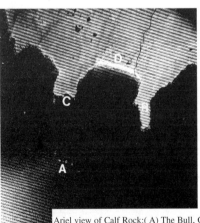

Ariel view of Calf Rock:(A) The Bull, Cow and Calf (B) Point Lance (C) Bull Island Point and (D) is the fishing community of Point Lance (once called Bull Cove), still viable today.

They voiced their complaint to the Newfoundland governor saying that, "The French constantly fish on our shore on Sundays, with boats from 60 to 100 in number. They have taken our dry fish from the beach, stolen the pickets from our graves for firewood and even threatened to shoot our people on our own ground. They have lately burnt a boat belonging to one of us and stolen a man's wharf posts which he had with difficulty procured at the distance of three miles."

In an effort to get the Newfoundland government to do something, several people of Lamaline sent a letter outlining the problem to his Excellency, the Governor of Newfoundland. These names were signed on the protest (with spelling as it appeared on the document):

Because of the conflict on the eastern side of the Burin Peninsula between the French fishermen and the English settlers the British eventually posted military personnel at Lamaline, hoping to prevent further problems with a foreign presence. Of course the sea still presented a danger to fishermen and to the military.

LAMALINE PROTESTERS, 1827	
Thomas Pitman	James Madigan
James Caines	William Pitman
Wm. Hooper	John Hillier
Stephen King	John Harnet
Saml. Daw	Thos. Purchase
Richard Cake	Robert Bonnell
George Caines	
Robert Hibditch, Constable	
James Crews, Constable	

On a Tuesday morning, August 29, 1843, the schooner *Customer* under Captain Keating left Lamaline for St. John's. It had a cargo of fish and oil and, in addition to his own crew, Keating had on board several of the officers and men of His Majesty's Ship (HMS) *Electra*. Lieutenant Dyett, along with several British military men, had spent the summer of 1843 in the Lamaline area, helping protect English fishing rights. With the summer fishery ending, Dyett's contingent returned to St. John's, perhaps to re-join HMS *Electra*.

On Wednesday night off the southern Avalon the *Customer* encountered a heavy gale from the north and, in the battering it took in the storm, ran aground on an isolated heap of granite off Bull Island Point and Point Lance on the southern Avalon

Avalon Peninsula. About two kilometers south of Bull Island Point are three rocks of black slate known as The Bull, Cow and Calf. These are extremely hazardous navigational hazards; more so in the days of sailing craft, perhaps without proper charts and maybe sailing at night. Today they are well-marked; in fact the local fishermen, especially those of St. Bride's are able to steam between the Bull and Calf whereas most navigators give them a wide clearance.

Customer's crew and passengers were now aground near "The Calf." They remained on the wreck for seven hours, taking the full brunt of wind and wave. Finally, by means of a rope to the shore, they succeeded in getting onto the Calf Rock, barren and desolate and with just enough surface area to allow a few men to stand.

They were on The Calf for two more hours with seas breaking over the crag. One person had already perished during the wreck or transfer to the isolated islet. Then when hope for survival of the others seemed at its lowest point, a boat belonging to Bartholomew (son of Daniel) Rourke of St. Mary's passed in the distance. Somehow the stranded men managed to signal Rourke. Rourke maneuvered as close to Calf Rock as possible and eventually succeeded in getting the stranded men off.

In St. John's Lieutenant Dyett went to media of the day to thank Bartholomew Rourke. In *The Royal Gazette* the headlines read **PROVIDEN-TIAL ESCAPE**, saying of the rescue:

Rourke incurred, as he did so, the greatest risk of his own life and property. The Officer and men of HMS *Electra* take this public opportunity of expressing their high sense of his daring intrepid-

On September 23, 1870, Commissioner of Wrecked Property Henry Benning notified the public that schooner *Vulture* was lost on Morgan's Island near Lamaline. Most of Ridley and Sons' cargo of lumber from Pugwash to Harbour Grace was saved.

ity, to which, in a main degree, they attribute the preservation of their lives. We trust he will be justly rewarded. We regret to add that one life was lost.

Neither Dyett nor the newspapers identified the person who perished in the shipwreck on the Calf Rock.

How a Dreaded Disease Reached Carbonear Island

Date:	*1865*
Location:	*Carbonear Island*
Fatalities:	*Many*
Remarks:	*Carbonear Ship Brings Smallpox*

In 1865 a ship brought a scourge, a dreaded disease, one which there was no cure for, to Carbonear. In the nineteenth century smallpox, which today has been eradicated, ran its course until many who had contracted the disease died. Ships which brought infectious diseases from other lands were required to raise a yellow flag and were not permitted in port. Homes which harbored these diseases - diphtheria, smallpox - were also put under quarantine.

The brig *Thomas Ridley* was built by Michael Kearney on Carbonear Beach and launched in February 1852. The best of

Photo of *Thomas Ridley* courtesy *Book of Newfoundland, volume four*

workmanship and much hardwood went into its construction. At 126 ton, *Thomas Ridley* was one of the largest vessels built for the Newfoundland seal hunt prior to the introduction of steam-powered vessels in the 1860s. For years it sailed under the Carbonear captains Nicholas Hanrahan, William Taylor and John Horwood. *Thomas Ridley* lasted thirty- three years until it was lost in a storm on the Labrador coast on October 13, 1885.

All ships, no matter how well built, undergo repairs and twice in its lifetime New Perlican's George Pittman, a well-known shipwright in his day, repaired *Thomas Ridley*. The brig was 24 feet wide and was over 12 feet deep in the holds. On the large cutwater stem it carried a figure head, not of a bird or a woman, the standard figure, but of a man standing with a beaver hat on his head. This represented Thomas Ridley, a valued employee of Rorke's business.

The *Ridley*, as it was commonly called, went through many trials and tribulations on the high seas during its journeys from Europe, the West Indies, to South America, and to the ice fields off Labrador in search of seals. No wreck or storm was as devastating in its final toll of death as what happened aboard *Ridley* in 1865.

Ariel view of Carbonear Island

That fall the brig bought the terrible disease smallpox from Ireland to Carbonear. The *Ridley* was not allowed at dockside, but was to be moored off on the ship quarantine grounds or as was commonly said in Carbonear "anchored out in the stream." There some of the crew died. They were buried on Carbonear Island in graves without headstones for according to local tradition no gravestones ever existed on the island.

Smallpox, a viral and highly contagious disease, was nearly always fatal. The virus can be carried in the air or spread by physical contact. The acute illness lasts about three weeks, an incubation stage, then comes high fever and an eruption of sores on the skin. Should the person recover, perhaps through some unknown reserves of strength, convalescence lasts another two to three weeks, but the skin will bear marks or "pocks."

In spite of all precautions, smallpox spread at Carbonear and during winter of 1865-66 several people died from the dreaded disease.

Perils of the Sea at Pass Island

Date: *10, 1884*
Location: *Pass Island*
Fatalities: *None*
Remarks: *American Ship Wrecked*
      on Pass Island

The exact origins of settlement at Pass Island, Hermitage Bay, are difficult to trace. What is certain is that in the era of sailing ships, the relatively isolated community had seen the ebb and flow of local and foreign vessels. It is well-documented the American fishing fleet visited the south coast regularly in late nineteenth and early twentieth century. They came not only to reap the bounty of the prolific offshore banks, but also to obtain supplies of bait, usually herring which at one time was an abundant species in Fortune and Hermitage Bay.

But in November 1894, the Gloucester fishing schooner *Magnolia* paid a brief visit to Pass Island for another reason - trouble at sea.

Pass Island, situated off the tip of the peninsula that separates Connaigre Bay and Hermitage Bay, was first noted by Captain James Cook in his 1763 survey map, saying English fishermen resided there. In Newfoundland's first *Census* of 1836, 56 people lived at Pass Island - families of Fudge, Piercey, Rideout, Simms, Spencer, and Stickland; the Bobbetts, Coopers, Crants and Touchings came later so that by 1874 the population had risen to 215 people. They were all hardworking and congenial people, ready to extend a friendly hand so long ago to stranded American visitors.

It started when *Magnolia* left Gloucester on November 2, 1894, for the Grand Banks on a voyage for halibut. Under command of Captain Mason, the 108-ton vessel carried eighteen men. It fished on the southern end of the Grand Banks until November 23, obtaining about 15,000 pound of fish. November on the Grand Banks means boisterous weather and rough seas and Mason brought *Magnolia* into Hermitage Bay to finish his catch in the more sheltered waters off the south coast. He reached Pass Island on November 27 and, as it was blowing hard and snowing, sailed for the nearest harbour for shelter.

Mason anchored safely outside and sent a boat to shore for a local pilot. One of the inhabitants of Pass Island came on board and tried to get *Magnolia* to a better position. When the anchor was lifted, winds and sea took control of the ship. As the schooner was being driven onto the shore, the eight dories fastened in their nest on deck were loosed from their stays by the seas sweeping over the deck. Each surging wave carried the dories back and forth over the deck.

One man named Murdock was severely injured and the steering wheel was wrenched out of the grip of the helmsman, P. Dillon, and bruised him about the chest and head. In fact, not one person aboard the schooner escaped without some injury, slight or severe, as they tried to control the loose dories on deck. It took a few anxious moments before two or three dories were secured and made ready by the ship's side.

When *Magnolia* hit the rocks, the cabin stove overturned and in a minute or so the cabin and all the vessel above water was one mass of flames. Within hours hardly a stick or stanchion stood above water to show where *Magnolia* had grounded.

On Pass Island in 1894 there were well over two hundred people. One of the most established fishermen was George Simms, who had ten children. Without hesitation, he invited the stranded men into his home and fed them with whatever provisions he had. It was late November and food supplies had to be nurtured carefully to make them last through the long winter ahead.

When the storm abated, Simms carried them to Harbour Breton, the chief port in the general area. There Magistrate Hubert attended to the shipwrecked sailors' needs. On December 1 the coastal steamer *Grand Lake* stopped at Harbour Breton, picked up the seamen and carried them to St. John's. The American Consul provided lodging in the Seaman's Institute or as it was commonly called, the Sailor's Home. *Magnolia*'s stranded crew was most vocal in their praise of Newfoundland hospitality at Harbour

Breton and the treatment aboard the coastal steamer. They could not say enough to praise Mr. Simms. He gave them all he had in his house during their brief stay there.

1884 Ad for Sailor's Home

Remote and relatively inaccessible even in good sailing weather, the Simms family and other residents of Pass Island must have been severely affected by the reduction of supplies and food during the brief but dramatic stopover of American fisherman during fall of 1894. Pass Island was resettled in the late 1974, and its people moved on to live in Hermitage and other south coast towns. Today the island is deserted, the people gone, but remnants of island stories, like when *Magnolia* made an unscheduled stop near its shores, live on.

Rose of Sharon, Lost at Cann Island

Date: 10, 1912
Location: Cann Island
Fatalities: None
Remarks: Newfoundland Ship Wrecked on Cann Island

While the wreck of schooner *Rose of Sharon* is not dramatic nor was there loss of life, it serves to illustrate the privations our ancestors endured trying to earn a living from the remorseless sea. Economic loss and personal setback came in all seasons for seamen, but it seemed most hard to bear just as the fishing season ended and there were a few dollars to be made and spent.

In the fall of 1912 the schooner *Rose of Sharon,* a biblical reference to a plant and found in the Song of Solomon, left the Labrador coast for Carbonear, Conception Bay. It sailed from Cape Charles, Labrador, with 420 quintals of fish on board. *Rose of Sharon*, under command of Captain Joseph Priddle, had a fine time along; that is, winds were favorable and the ship made good speed, but in Stag Harbour Run conditions soon changed. Stag Harbour Run, lying off on the southern shore of Fogo Island, was known as an especially tricky passage, not to be attempted unless conditions were favorable. But Captain Priddle wished to make the sheltered harbor of Seldom-Come-By.

Owned by G. Soper and Sons of Carbonear, *Rose of Sharon* carried 10 crew and passengers, all of whom belonged to Carbonear and vicinity: Captain Priddle, the captain's wife and his eleven-year-old daughter Florence, William Long, George Rumsen, Arthur Winsor, George Barnes, William Barnes, Michael Murray, and Elsie Rossiter .

At 9 a.m. Friday, Priddle was negotiating the many crags and islands that dot Stag Harbour Run when the wind came up and the sea began to toss ominously. As Priddle was beating up

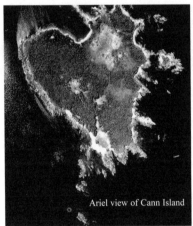

Ariel view of Cann Island

the run, the wheel chains gave out. Before anyone could do anything about the problem, *Rose of Sharon* was hard and fast upon a reef off Cann Island.

The schooner began to pound against the rocks and all realized that to stay aboard meant death. It was equally plain to see that to launch the two lifeboats in the white surf crashing against the rocks was risky.

But launching the lifeboats was their only alternative. The two women and the girl went in the captain's boat with some of the crew; the remaining crew went in the other. Time and time again while pulling for the shore, both boats were nearly swamped and everyone aboard was drenched with spray. All had to bail continuously and quickly for their lives depended on it.

Once the lifeboats grounded on the beach rocks, the men jumped out to their waist in water and had to carry Mrs. Priddle and her daughter in their arms. They realized they were on Cann Island, not far from Seldom-Come-By and Little Seldom.

At one time the island was inhabited. An October 1883 issue of *The Twillingate Sun* reports that on October 14 Captain John Normore of Cann Island left in his vessel the *Jenny* to sail to Hall's Bay, eighty miles westward. Four days later, off Fortune Harbour a gale carried away his mainsail.

Normore decided to shelter in Fortune Harbour, but the wind was against him and the *Jenny* began to drift out of control. But for some Fortune Harbour fishermen who towed the craft into harbour, it was felt Normore would have been lost. At the time the captain was about 50 years old and had lived on Cann Island most of his life.

Cann Island is easily reached from Little Seldom. Today people often rowed there to pick bakeapples. Small and treeless, it was often frequented by summertime berry pickers who walk around the island marshes and bogs looking for bakeapples. Tinker Rock, a smaller crag and more dangerous to shipping, lies close by. The waters off Cann Island and Tinker Island nearby saw much sea traffic in the days of sail. At least one ship in recent memory sank off Tinker - the salt-laden *Sally Irene*.

For *Rose of Sharon*'s compliment, now stranded on Cann Island, it was a matter of a wait before someone saw them and took them off. Boats were useless in such breakers, so they pulled them up to the high water mark and prepared to wait for rescue. All day Friday it was cold, but Friday night the wind increased. They had no food with them and the pangs of hunger were added to the pain of cold and exposure. Several times Friday night the stranded people tried to build a fire, but the hurricane of wind scattered the burning wood.

All night they walked and kept moving to increase the circulation of blood. Some parts of old sails that were aboard the

41

boats were fastened to the trees and this provided a temporary shelter. The two women and the young girl suffered the most in their wet clothing.

Saturday morning before daylight the S.S. *Fogota* anchored in the run and someone aboard saw a flickering fire *Rose of Sharon*'s crew were trying to light. Captain Barbour sent over a crew to pick up the hapless and shivering castaways. Aboard the steamer the crew gave them every attention.

That morning some clothing was salvaged from the wreck and about 20 quintals of fish, but the *Rose of Sharon* was never refloated. The side was torn out and the schooner filled with water; fortunately owner Soper had his ship insured through the Conception Bay Mutual Insurance Plan.

Fogota landed the shipwrecked mariners in Seldom. In time they made their way to Lewisporte to make connections with the eastbound train to Carbonear.

The "Other" Penguin Islands

Date:	*04, 1895*
Location:	*Penguin Island*
Fatalities:	*One*
Remarks:	*Nova Scotia Ship Wrecked on Penguin Island*

There are two groups of Penguin Islands off Newfoundland. Those at the North East coast near the Straight Shore are well-known and many stories of shipwrecks take their origins from those two islands, North Penguin and South Penguin. The second set, consisting of about 20 islands, islets and crags, are located about 12 kilometers from the South Coast off Cape LaHune.

Although a few good ships and men have been lost there, they are more obscure. Perhaps one factor is that there is less sea traffic for the islands are situated well away from a land mass and any major port or harbour.

About 1915 a lighthouse was established on this island. This was a "manned" light until about the year 2000. For many years the light keeper was Wallace McDonald. But this tale of woe though takes place before there was a light on Penguin Islands. In the darkness of a late April night in 1895, trouble loomed for Captain R. H. Tobin of North Sydney. He came home on May 8 and related the odd tale of why he had arrived without his schooner *Freddie Walter*.

Captain Tobin left St. Pierre on April 19 for North Sydney. He had no cargo aboard, except rock ballast to keep his schooner steady in case he met adverse winds off Newfoundland's South Coast. On a Tuesday morning, a strong wind from the southwest came on. The pumps choked and Tobin thought it best to head for the nearest safe harbour, Burgeo. He was then about 80 miles out from St. Pierre.

Then he and his crew figured the weather and winds were too strong to make Burgeo and shaped a course for Miquelon. By the time the pumps were free, the wind veered southerly, increasing to gale force. In the storm the foresail was blown away and the crew bent on the storm try sail in its place. Tobin went below to his cabin to take off his course, but while there he heard one of the crew shout, "Breakers!"

Penguin Islands off Cape LaHune. The large island is Harbour Island with the lighthouse. There are at least a dozen or more large and small islets and crags here. Seamen give this treacherous area wide berth.

He rushed on deck, threw the wheel to port, but was a minute too late - *Freddie Walter* hit the western end of the Penguin Islands. The captain shouted for the men to stand by the ship, but one fellow, Thomas Power of Placentia, Newfoundland, was the first to jump for the rock. He slipped and was not seen afterward.

Two other crew jumped and landed safely. There were two left aboard - Captain Tobin and another deck hand. Within a

43

moment the schooner lurched off the rock and began to drift and sink rapidly. A half a mile further down the Tobin could see a break in the rocks which might provide some shelter. The schooner reached the spot, but sank to the sheer poles.

Tobin and the other man climbed the rigging and stayed there 48 hours. *Freddie Walter* struck at 10:30 a.m. Tuesday, April 23. The first night they were in the rigging, the bottom was torn out of the vessel.

The two men stranded on a rock would have perished, except the wind diminished and the breakers subsided; otherwise they would have been washed off their perch.

Fishermen from Cape LaHune frequent the prolific waters around the Penguin Islands and when the heavy weather abated, went to the area. In the morning of Thursday, April 25, they saw the shipwrecked men and, using lifeline to haul them through the water, took them off.

Captain Tobin returned to North Sydney and had to relate the tale of how he lost his schooner at the Penguin Islands, but more traumatic, how the wreck resulted in the death of one of his crew.

NEWFOUNDLAND
Notice to Mariners
(No. 7, 1915)

Penguin Island, South West Coast
FOG ALARM ESTABLISHED
Lat. 46. 22. 50 N. Approx.
Lon. 50. 58. 50. W. Approx.

POSITION—On the highest part of the Island.

DESCRIPTION — 3 inch Diaphone operated by air compressed by oil engine.

PERIODS—2 Blasts in every 90 sec. ends thus:

BLAST. Silent. BLAST. Silent.
2 Sec. 10 Sec. 2 Sec. 76 Sec.

STRUCTURES—Engine house, Keeper's dwelling and Store house, each one storey flat-roofed.

COLOURS—White and Black vertical stripes on each building.

REMARKS— During this season an Occulting White Dioptric Light of the 4th Order will be established in a lantern erected on the roof of Engine House. Periods of which will be 5 seconds alternate light and eclipse. Visible in all directions.

Authority—Inspector of Lighthouses.

ALAN GOODRIDGE,
Deputy Minister Marine & Fisheries
ept. Marine

Notice of establishment of fog alarm. In 1915 this public announcement says a fog alarm has been established on the Penguin Islands and under the section "Remarks", that a light will be put there in the fall of 1915.

Playing Sad Havoc with the Cromwell Line

Date: 09,1883
Location: St. Mary's Bay
Fatalities: None
Remarks: Wreck of "Canima"

On the morning of September 6,1883, the 45 crew and 14 passengers of the Cromwell Line S.S. *Canima* ended up standing for several hours on Gull Island, a rock off Gull Island Point in St. Mary's Bay. Luckily the seas were calm in the early morning daylight and that enabled the people of Peter's River to get to the island.

There was a time in Newfoundland's marine history when the Cromwell Line ran a freight and passenger service to St. John's from Halifax and New York. The Cromwell Line was established by the American businessman H. B. Cromwell initially to serve Savannah and New York. He expanded the line to other ports including a New York to Halifax to St. John's triangular service in 1874.

However, the Newfoundland run was nothing but one ship disaster after another, prompting a reporter to say that the Cromwell Line steamers "have won a most unenviable reputation and almost, if not altogether, upon Newfoundland's coasts. The *George Washington* and *George Cromwell* are names fraught with sad memories."

Two sister ships, S.S. *George Washington* and *George Cromwell*, disappeared in early 1877 near Cape Race. On January 20 S.S. *George Washington*, plying between Halifax and St. John's, was lost with all crew and passengers a half mile west of Mistaken Point, near Cape Race. It carried eight passengers, twenty-three crew and a full load of barrels of flour, pork and general merchandise.

The 972-ton *George Cromwell* left Halifax for St. John's on January 31, 1877, and seemingly vanished. Days later its wreckage was located at Golden Bay, leading mariners to think it ran upon the treacherous St. Mary's Keys. No one survived. Listed in the roster of the lost was a Newfoundland crewman and two (of seven passengers) were from St. John's. In addition to these two devastating catastrophes, the Cromwell Line also lost the S.S. *Cortes* between Halifax and St. John's.

An iron screw steamer built in Scotland in 1873, the 546-ton *Canima* left Halifax on Monday September 3, 1883, for St. John's. Captain James A. Farquhar was in command and carried a cargo of flour, beef and pork. Many passengers were from Newfoundland or New York. The next report of the ship was, "*Canima* lost at St. Shotts. Crew and passengers saved."

Actually it struck Gull Island at the entrance to St. Mary's Bay, several miles west of St. Shotts. The island, which supports a few tuffs of grass, is about 12 feet wide, 40 feet long and quite high. It's close to land, yet no vessels can go around it as a narrow gulch separates the crag from land.

Peering through fog on Thursday morning September 6, Captain Farquhar saw the St. Mary's Light and took his course off from it, going one point further south to avoid the very rocks which claimed his ship. But no satisfactory explanation - excessive tide into the bay or if *Canima*'s compass was out - was offered for the ship ending up on Gull Island. The steamer was seven miles off course.

Shipping authorities were also mystified on the excessive length of time, one and a half hours, it took to launch the steamer's lifeboats. Had the seas been high, it could have resulted in the loss of every person on board. There were reports of "an utter lack of discipline and the commonest precautions being neglected at the launching of the boats."

The blame for the latter could only be placed on agencies which select steamers' crews

Vessels lost on or near Gull Island, St. Mary's Bay

M.H. Carter, September 6, 1868

S.S. Canima September 6, 1883, all survived

Robert Low 1885?, some survived

brigantine *Isabel* February 22, 1887, no survivors

Lantana December 20, 1890, no survivors

S.S. Helgoland January 11, 1900, no survivors

Baden Powell March 25, 1908, crew rowed to Trepassey

S.S. Twekesbury March 1920, crew rowed into Peter's River.

and the training they received. One newspaper, in commenting of the loss of *Canima*, said:

> ...the lifeboats are a show to deceive the unwary into the belief that they would be safe in case of an accident to the steamer. The boats are seldom moved from their places and many a so-called sailor on board a steamer is an utter stranger to their management. As for the Cromwell ships, a sinister fatality seems to have marked out this line, and to be playing sad havoc with its boats. (The *Morning Herald Halifax*, September 25, 1883)

Now all aboard the S.S. *Canima* were at the mercy of the lifeboats and the sailors manning them. According to the September 7 and 8 editions of *The New York Times* "the passengers and crew had to leap for their lives - and some passengers were dragged ashore on the island by ropes." Fortunately in the calm seas they were all landed on Gull Rock, saving absolutely nothing; no luggage, extra clothes, food or water, or even a piece of canvas to shelter them.

The nearest town, about three miles east, is Peter's River, in Holyrood Bay at the eastern entrance to St. Mary's Bay. Livyers there soon learned of the wreck and on Thursday evening went to aid the stricken band of shipwrecked people. In the 1880s the population of Peter's River stood at no more four or five homes and no more than twenty or thirty people; thus the number of small boats and provisions available to succor *Canima*'s contingent of souls was limited. It is likely they helped getting lines and then the people from the stricken ship to the small island.

Early Friday morning, after nearly a day on the barren rock, Captain A. Larder in his schooner *Thistle* went to Gull Island to bring the castaways to the mainland. In the evening the Newfoundland steamer *Cabot* sailed to St. Mary's Bay to transport them to St. John's.

The hulk of S.S. *Canima* was sold at public auction a couple of weeks later, "as is and where is." Only one man put in a bid - 20 dollars - and he got the wreck although it is not known what he did with the hulk afterwards, but he certainly lost no money on the purchase.

Some of the passengers involved in *Canima*'s traumatic wreck were Mrs. Campion, Reverend A.C.T. Wood, John

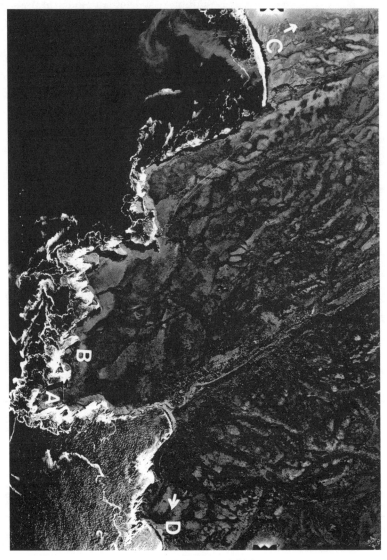

Ariel shot of Gull Island and vicinity.

Gull Island (A) and Gull Island Point (B). Whitecaps break against a rugged land and high cliffs. A narrow chasm - a little more than 100 feet wide and 150 feet deep - separates the island from land. Several ships were wrecked on this outcrop over the years. Peter's River (C) is just up the coast; St. Shotts (D) lies to the east.

McCardle, T. D. Lane, H. F. Adams, Alfred B. Scott, J. F. Goodrich, Miss M. Riley, Thomas Greaves, Mrs. Greaves, the son of Mr. J.T. Wood, W.F. Harper and Henry S. Harper. The latter two were sons of one of the members of the well-known publishing house Harper and Sons (today's HarperCollins) of New York.

Author's Note: I became aware of *Canima*'s loss from Lee Harper, grandson of Henry Harper, and Lee sent additional details of his grandfather's experience. Henry was 19 at the time of the wreck of *Canima*. Perhaps his experiences in defying death on the ocean were lessons well-learned for on the night of April 14-15, 1912, he was aboard the *Titanic*. It struck an iceberg and sank in the Atlantic (about 153 kilometers south of Newfoundland and Gull Island, St. Mary's Bay, where Henry had been shipwrecked many years before). Of the 2200 people aboard *Titanic*, a little over 700 survived. Henry Harper was one of them.

Chapter 3
Castaways and Survivors

In 1930 the schooner *Carranza* was accosted by a heavy wind storm accompanied by lightning. When a gust of wind hit the sails and at the same time lightning struck the mainmast, the vessel capsized. Within a minute it went to the bottom, taking the captain and nine others with it. Miraculously six others reached a dory. They had nothing except their lives and a will to live - no compass, light, oars, water, food or any other necessity of life. A section of the story of the 72-hour fight for survival says:

"They headed the small craft into the wind and set their course by the North Star, which they could see occasionally. Their plan was to try to stay in the shipping lane. Sooner or later a ship would possibly come by. If they could stay afloat and not die from hunger and thirst, they would survive." Taken from *Lost at Sea- A Compilation* (2001).

These are the stories of shipwrecked persons; those who find themselves thrust into the elements with little or no aids to reach help. A popular song of survivors and castaways says:

Pull for the shore, sailor, pull for the shore!
Heed not the rolling waves, but bend to the oar;
 Safe in the life boat, sailor, cling to self no more!
Leave the poor old stranded wreck, and pull for the shore.

Philip P. Bliss, 1873

And those words describe what happened to the Gallop men in story three, "To Sleep; To Dream; To Survive." That story is one of my favorites for another reason. Many years ago, perhaps in the late 1700s, William Gallop deserted a British warship and settled in Fortune. In time one of his children married a Forsey from Grand Bank, a distant maternal relative of mine. Some of the Gallop descendants eventually migrated to Codroy and that's where the story takes place.

As well, I have heard of the legend of Pope's Harbour, Trinity Bay, stemming back perhaps before the mid-nineteenth century. There's little for a full-fledged tale but, according to the story, a fishing vessel left a crew member ashore near Pope's Harbour, intending to return later. The ship sailed away and was never heard of again; perhaps lost with all hands. The man left behind had no supplies, food, shelter, but for a cave near the harbour. Local residents still point out the cave where the man slowly starved to death. Who was around to tell his sad story is a mystery, but his remains were found in that cave.

Our hardy ancestors. They eked out their existence on the edge of the ocean; some of them were truly castaways and survivors.

Horror off the Coast

Date: 04, 1897
Location: On the Grand Banks
Fatalities: 62
Remarks: French Ship Strikes an Iceberg

Danger to ships and men on the high seas in the days of wooden schooners and canvas sail were many: heavy seas, high winds, fire, fog-enshrouded coasts, partially-submerged derelicts, grounding on treacherous shoals and hidden rocks, and, in wartime, the actions of enemy ships and submarines.

Another silent enemy were the icebergs and the deadly collisions with low-lying pans of ice. Many a ship and all crew disappeared after running into ice; the luckier ones were those ships where a few survived to tell the tale. Bergs don't usually reach the waters between Cape Race and St. Pierre; usually they drift farther out into the Atlantic where they slowly melt.

In the spring of 1897 the French brigantine *Valliant* sailed for St. Pierre. Aboard were 74 St. Malo fishermen and crew ready to pursue the summer's voyage off Newfoundland or to collect bait near Miquelon. In the night of Wednesday, April 14, it struck a low-lowing iceberg on the Grand Banks.

The ship was under full sail, traveling at top speed, and the impact was so great, it threw everyone out of their bunk. The yards fell as the masts broke. *Valliant*'s stem and bow were split asunder and the hold quickly flooded. The ship sank in twenty minutes.

Some men were severely injured in the collision; many drowned by the inrush of water or were killed by falling timbers or spars. Others drowned while trying the leave the ship in dories. In retrospect, these may have been the lucky ones, for what followed for the survivors who made it to sea in small boats was an odyssey of horror and death. The screams and shouts which accompanied the sinking of *Valliant* proved only too clearly several went down with the ship.

Many who reached the deck wore only night garments, and saw that damage to the ship was such it would not float many minutes. The mere launch of dories, which many fishermen had done quickly and efficiently often in the past, brought out vile instincts. There were seven dories, usually taking two to four men each and two small lifeboats - the latter were smashed and useless. The number of boats undamaged was not sufficient for all and a vicious battle for places in a boat broke out.

One boat with seven men and the bosun - Noel Maubeche who took charge - drifted away from the wreck. The bosun was well-dressed, but the others had little or no clothes and no food. They had no boots, only sabots, wooden shoes, and no socks. They had pushed off from the wreck so quickly, they neglected to take sails, oars, provisions or water.

April on the waters off Newfoundland is a cold, raw time, temperatures drop to near freezing and often below. Any who made it to a boat suffered untold agonies of cold, hunger and thirst. For the four days they were adrift in this frail little craft, every sea swept over it, drenching the occupants to the skin and forcing them to bail. They bailed until they were too feeble to throw out any more water and didn't care if they perished or not.

For warmth, they packed themselves closely along the bottom, but in the keen frost and drift ice, which at times surrounded the craft, there was no way they could keep warm. Gnawing pangs of hunger grew more intense by the hour. Thus they suffered, until death claimed two. On the second day out, the survivors threw the bodies overboard and, a few hours later, saw another boat from *Valliant*.

It was the captain with several men and they too had no oars or provisions. He also reported a dead man aboard. Gradually they drifted apart. By the third day Maubeche lost a third man by death, and that night the famished survivors cut some strips of flesh from the corpse and appeased their hunger.

On the morning of the fourth day they further devoured it and by the evening, when they were rescued, the body was half consumed. Captain Eve and the French fishing ship *Victor Eugene* accidentally stumbled upon the drifting boat. Eve and the crew of the rescue ship were so horrified at the sight, they sank the body and the boat at once.

The four living men - Maubeche, Marie Agennis, W. Boulanger and Alf. Nonyon - had lost all reason and were so exhausted that had to be lifted over the ship's side swathed in blankets. Their bodies were masses of white, frost-bitten flesh. When found they were all lying unconscious on the bottom of the boat awash in six inches of cold water. They could not stand or speak for twelve days.

After cruising around for two days searching for other boats, *Victor Eugene* reached St. Pierre-Miquelon on April 27. *Valliant*'s survivors had to be carried ashore on stretchers; limbs were useless and amputations were necessary. One of the four did not live; others lost arms and legs, some had to have their ears and noses removed.

It was thought no one else had survived. Ice must have crushed the small boats or heavy storms would have sunk them. Authorities in St. Pierre made contact with a sealing vessel from St. John's to steam to the site where *Valliant* went down to search for others.

Another chapter in the harrowing story of *Valliant* opened and closed on May 1. The brigantine *Amedee* arrived in St. Pierre with four more survivors. They had been in the largest boat *Valliant* carried and had 21 souls aboard when it left the wreck.

Like the other boats, it too was launched in haste and the men crowded into it after a desperate fight on deck. Most had little clothing. For six days they drifted without oars or sail and every day their numbers decreased. The cold was so intense, that even the sailors on *Amedee* said it was hard to stand on deck with several overcoats on.

Fortunately this group had a source of food - the ship's dog which had jumped in the boat with them. When they could no longer endure the pangs of hunger, they killed it and kept a vital spark inside them alive. After the second day and night, the weaker ones began to succumb. Consumption of human flesh was not attempted in this boat, for they had a little food and the bodies had to thrown over the side to keep the lifeboat lightened and above water.

Every few hours the numbers alive decreased; others threw the bodies overboard, first taking any outer garments for themselves. Yet the boat was so overcrowded, half of them had to lie on the bottom while the others occupied the thwarts, reversing the positions every few hours. This gave them some sleep for all, but the salt spray coming over the boat froze solidly after night-

THE EVENING HERALD, ST. JOHNS, NEWFOUNDLAND

The St. Pierre Tragedy
FOUR MORE RESCUED.
SEVENTEEN DIE OF COLD
Another Harrowing Tale
OF SUFFERING & DEATH.

Six Days Adrift Witho— Sustained by Eating— pected to Live.--Unco—

THE EVENING HERALD, ST. JOHNS, NEWFOUNDLA

They Ate Human Flesh
An Ocean Tragedy
SEVENTY SOULS SACRIFICED
ONLY FOUR SAVED

A Thrilling Tale of Suffering & Death--The French Barquentine "Valliant" Strikes An Iceberg & Sinks--Seventy of Her Passengers and Crew Perish--One of The Most Awful Marine Horrors on Record.

The *Evening Herald* April 29 and May 3, 1897, show the depth of horror and tragedy that happened off the coast of Newfoundland with the loss of *Valliant*.

fall. They were thus encased in a shroud of ice. All were frost-bitten, until death ended sufferings.

Several went mad from the misery of the situation and the thought of no rescue. The few who escaped this danger had much trouble preventing others from overturning the boat or from attempting some other senseless action.

In the last 36 hours the few remaining survivors were only partly conscious of their surroundings. They, too, lay in the bottom of the boat, soaked, cold and with no more food left. They gave up any hope of recovery.

At 10 p.m. on April 20, six days after leaving the wreck, one of the four remaining fortunately awoke and, looking over the side, saw a light. He roused the others and they united their shout in one voice. Someone aboard the brig *Amedee* heard it. So close was the brig, its wash nearly swamped the lifeboat.

The four survivors were tenderly cared for aboard the brig, but within a few days all had to have their legs amputated above the knees. Many also lost their hands. Except for the first boat rescued, which had briefly encountered the captain's small boat, no other dories were seen. There were no other survivors. Of *Valliant*'s compliment of 70, eight made it to land, seven lived to sail back to France.

All in all a terrible tale of suffering, one hardly paralleled, in the waters off our coast in the days of sail.

Pull for the Shore

Date:	*05, 1909*
Location:	*Off Newfoundland*
Fatalities:	*None*
Remarks:	*Newfoundland Seamen Adrift*

There was quite a crowd standing on the St. John's waterfront premises of Alan Goodridge & Sons about eight p.m. on May 29, 1909. A lifeboat could be seen slowly coming through the Narrows. As more people gathered, speculation began as to who the occupants were and to what ship the lifeboat belonged.

As it drew closer, some people who knew the markings on the lifeboat said it belonged to Goodridge's schooner *Electra*.

Others in the crowd knew that ship was commanded by Captain Cave and it was due in port about this time. But what had become of the *Electra* and could it be that *Electra*'s crew was in the lifeboat? As the boat drew near, someone recognized Cave in the stern, steering. In a few minutes the boat reached the wharf.

Then it was learned *Electra* had sunk, but the crew was all accounted for and in relatively good shape. Later that evening, a curious reporter visited Captain Cave at his home on Leslie Street and Cave told him the story.

Electra, built in Jersey in 1854, was 165 gross ton. It was 118 feet long and 26 feet wide. The vessel had been brought to Newfoundland a few years previously; by then it was already over fifty years old. The Goodridges, who had begun their business in Renews prior to 1840 and eventually expanded to St. John's, needed another foreign-going ship, purchased *Electra*. They put Cave in command and his crew was his son and first mate Bert Cave, bosun Ambrose King, cook Martin Billard, seamen Thomas Croucher, Thomas Philpott, John Dazzle, a colored man and Alexander Wentzel. Except for Wentzel, who belonged to Belgium, most resided in St. John's.

Electra, laden with salt and 20 puncheons of wine for the Goodridge business, left Oporto on March 23, 1909. Weather was fine for a week or so, but then the heavy weather came on - gale after gale. Three times the ship was driven back to a previous position. As Cave remembered:

> The seas we encountered during the storm rolled mountains high and carried away part of the bulwarks, as well as damaging other parts of the ship. We "hove to" for 85 hours with the sails lashed. Drags and oil bags, which we put out, kept *Electra* from drifting too much to the leeward.
> We got into fields of ice on April 26 and at 2:30 that afternoon the vessel got into a heavy jam. This twisted the bow and stern so badly that it was impossible to do anything to keep it afloat. Water rushed into the hold and the pumps were worked to try and keep the boat afloat.

Cave said that during this storm he lost a small dog overboard which he was bringing home to his daughter. By now, all the crew realized it was impossible to keep the schooner afloat any longer. They also knew their position was several miles off Newfoundland's coast. To delay sinking for a few hours, perhaps until winds pitched down, Cave ordered the ship lightened.

One of the crew was sent into the hold to smash out the heads of the wine puncheons. Precious cargo poured into the bilges and for awhile the pumps drew water and wine. But the plan worked. *Electra*'s hull rose a few inches above the water line, giving the vessel a few more hours grace.

It gave the crew time to collect a few articles of clothes, to provision two boats and to launch them over the side. As this work finished and the boats were in the water *Electra* gave its final plunge, downward head foremost to her last resting place on the ocean floor.

They all got in the larger lifeboat, towing the small boat behind them. The latter was leaky and had the bottom covered with canvas but, fearing it might be needed, Captain Cave decided to tow it astern. They all worked with a will at the oars and sail, but Cave never released his hold on the tiller until the boat touched Goodridge's wharf. While the others managed a cat nap for an hour or two, Cave, according to the story to newspaper reporters, never slept a wink.

They worked the lifeboat closer to land, sometimes going through slob ice for miles, but in clear water they made good progress. The captain continued:

> [We] had plenty of provisions. Alan Goodridge &
> Sons had well-supplied the *Electra* with food,
> enough on board to last six months. However, we
> did not have hot drink and there was no means of
> making a fire to make any. Two of the crew
> became delirious for a short time.
> No sail was sighted since we left the spot were
> *Electra* went down until entering the Narrows,
> when we saw a northern craft entering port too.

Another odd thing about it was that while we were in the lifeboat, numerous sea birds followed the boat for miles.

Cave lost several nautical instruments, but saved his two sextants and two charts. The crew lost their personal belongings. Seaman Thomas Croucher, who lived in St. John's, said: "As I got ashore I was met by an old friend, James Murphy who worked for the St. John's City Council, and a few of us shipwrecked men were taken up to Strang's for a good hot rum and lemon."

Shipwreck was nothing new for Captain Cave. During his 47 years of going to sea, he had several unusual experiences. He was shipwrecked off the coast of China thirty years prior to the loss of *Electra*. When the English vessel he was on went down, he spent 18 days in an open boat, coasting along the waterways off China before rescue. Four or five years previous to 1909 he was on *Gladiola* when it was lost eighteen miles off Brazil. He was also on the *Mistletoe* when that schooner was crushed by ice, abandoned and the crew taken to Philadelphia.

A Great Jervois Man, Sole Survivor

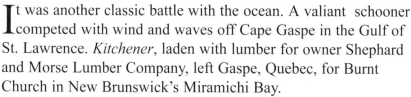

Date:	10,1931
Location:	Bonaventure Island
Fatalities:	2
Remarks:	Newfoundland Seaman Survives Shipwreck

It was another classic battle with the ocean. A valiant schooner competed with wind and waves off Cape Gaspe in the Gulf of St. Lawrence. *Kitchener*, laden with lumber for owner Shephard and Morse Lumber Company, left Gaspe, Quebec, for Burnt Church in New Brunswick's Miramichi Bay.

Captain David S. Miller of Alberton, PEI, was in command and his two seamen were Harry Clarey of Arichat, Nova Scotia, and John Skinner of Great Jervois in Hermitage Bay,

Newfoundland. Miller sailed into a mid-October storm in the Gulf and soon the pounding caused severe leaks in the schooner. By the next day seams opened; water poured in faster than the three men could pump it out. *Kitchener* was foundering.

On Saturday, October 17, Captain Miller and his two crew decided to abandon ship on a raft constructed of lengths of lumber and deck fittings. Possibly the small dory or lifeboat had been swept away or smashed in the high seas.

During the storm, Miller and Clarey washed off the raft and drowned. Skinner found that extra reserve of strength, held on and drifted onto Bonaventure Island where he clung to life Saturday night, all Sunday until Monday morning. He was found by fishermen and taken to the village of Perce, Quebec.

Clarey's remains were recovered on October 20. Captain Miller, about 70 years old, left a wife in Alberton and had five daughters and three sons. Miller's father, from Scotland, had also been a sea captain and lost his life to the sea many years before.

Both the Moncton paper *The Daily Times* and Newfoundland's *The Evening Telegram* feature the amazing story of John Skinner, sole survivor.

A Disastrous Spring

Date: 05,1887
Location: In Trinity Bay
Fatalities: 5
Remarks: Collision between "Plover" and "Trixie H"

By late May of 1887, most shipowners and seamen were aware of the several recent disasters that had recently occurred on Newfoundland's shores. One public statement said, "It has been our painful task to chronicle several marine casualties, all of which have loss of life." In March the barquentine *Susan* collided with an iceberg and five lives were lost. Steamer *John Knox* was wrecked at Channel on May 1 and all 29 aboard perished.

The first knowledge of another calamity came at 10 a.m. on May 22. It was then the northern coastal steamer *Plover*, Captain Manuel, came in through St. John's narrows and into port. Crowded on its foredeck stood a group of shipwrecked mariners. When *Plover* tied up, it was quickly learned they were the survivors of the schooner *Trixie H*.

Trixie H was owned in Heart's Content and skippered at that time by Captain Robert Piercey. It had left St. John's the previous morning, May 21, bound for home. There were 19 passengers and crew aboard - sixteen men and three women. Ten o'clock that night, when the schooner was about halfway between Old Perlican and Trinity, the S.S. *Plover* ran into the schooner.

At the time of the collision, the wind blew a stiff breeze for the north

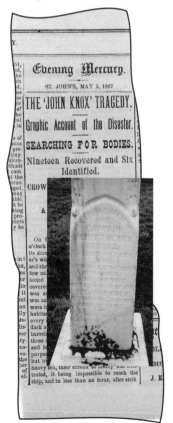

The stone immortalizing the loss of *John Knox* at Channel-Port aux Basques reads: Captain Robert Henry Brolly, aged 34 years, who with his entire crew of 29 souls was drowned at the wreck of the S.S. *John Knox* at Channel Harbor, May 1, 1887

61

northeast, the sea was smooth, but the night was pitch black. *Plover*, steaming along at about seven knots, had a small boat in tow. Only one person aboard the steamer heard or saw another ship; then it was too late - there was a grinding jar and Captain Manuel ran onto the bridge. He ordered the engines reversed, his crew stood to the rail with lines and also lowered ropes down over the side in case someone in the water reached the side of the steamer. Some of *Plover*'s boats were lowered.

It was later learned the schooner had been struck on the starboard bow. As *Trixie H* lay more or less flat on its side, many passengers were clinging to the port side. These were quickly transferred to the steamer.

One woman, Mary Coombs, was rescued. When she was taken from the water, she was unconscious, nearly frozen, and only partially clad. Ishmael Branton, who was in the water the longest, was rescued by Captain Manuel, who jumped over the side the reach the drowning man. Several others from *Trixie H* clambered in over the bow of the steamer unassisted.

The collision happened so quickly Captain Piercey and the men on deck of *Trixie H* did not have time to warn those below deck in the forecastle or the three men and three women in the cabin. Those on deck were unable to get the schooner's boat off deck.

When Captain Piercey and others checked to see who was missing, five could not be accounted for. His two brothers and his sister were gone: William Piercey, aged 28, married with two children, James Piercey, aged 18 and Anna Maria Piercey, aged 25. Mrs. Eliza Wadham had drowned; she was married, but had no children. Richard Rockwood, a young man who had for some time been a member of the police force in St. John's, was also listed among the dead. He had recently resigned

Evening Mercury.

ST. JOHNS, MAY 23, 1887

RELIEF WORK—THEIR PERILS AND DIFFICULTIES.

DISASTROUS COLLISION.

A SCHOONER CUT DOWN BY THE S. S. "PLOVER."

FIVE LIVES LOST.

his position as a policeman to work in the summer's fishery out of Heart's Content.

When the circumstances of the collision were recounted afterwards, it was known many passengers were below and probably asleep at the time of the accident. Most rushed on deck without coats and some without trousers or shoes. The captain's sister was last seen on the cabin floor, screaming.

It was difficult to determine which ship was at fault. *Trixie H* had all lights burning and the helmsman, John Clarke, had seen the lights of the steamer before the collision. Clarke vowed he called out two or three times to those on board the steamer as it came near to the schooner. No one heard this.

It was determined that Captain Manuel was asleep below at the time and second officer Batterton was in charge. Batterton later claimed he had gone below for a few minutes. *Plover*'s helmsman saw the schooner's lights moments before collision but, without commands from the captain or first officer, had not made any attempt to stop the steamer's engine until Manuel came on deck after the hit.

Later at the Court of Inquiry the survivors testified that Captain Manuel had done all he could to save lives. They spoke in highest terms of his kindness and of the promptness with which his crew effected a rescue.

Rescued from *Trixie H*, May 21, 1887. Most were from Heart's Content and vicinity:	
Capt Robert Piercey	John Clarke
Jonas Seward	Alfred Surey (Churley?)
Levi Williams	John Miles
Jethro Penny	Alex Dwyer
William Warren	Martin Snook
Thomas Conway	Ishmael Branton
Fred Genge	Mary Coombs

The German Immigrants at Cape Race

Date:	*08,1840*
Location:	*Cape Race and Renews*
Fatalities:	*50*
Remarks:	*German Immigrant Ship Wrecked at Cape Race*

A young man from Germany narrowly escaped death in a ship-wreck at Cape Race, but his wife and five children perished in the wreck.

On June 30, 1840, Philip Meisenheimer and his young family boarded the brig *Florence* at Rotterdam in the Netherlands. They, along with 75 other passengers, left Germany - then a country composed of many fractious city states, heading for New York. Many wished for a better life in America; other immigrants left their homeland to avoid the conflicts and strife raging between the various kingdoms and states in Germany, still in a state of feudal warfare. The war lords had a habit of conscripting young sons to fight for their city and fathers went to great lengths to keep their offspring safe.

Ariel shot of Cape Race

Before making the long journey, many of the German passengers sold everything they had and converted their savings and assets into gold or silver. To hide this - their only worldly possessions - they strapped the gold around their waists or had it sewn into their clothes.

Florence, commanded by Captain Sam Rose of the United States, had eight crew. Meisenheimer's family and the other passengers had a pleasant voyage until August 9 when they were off Cape Race and surrounded by thick fog. Without warning *Florence* was swept onto the rocks somewhere between Cripple

Cove and Money Cove, Cape Race.

The ship was fast breaking up. Many took a chance and jumped into the water for their lives. Those who could not swim struggled between the surging tides and rocks. Others, perhaps better swimmers, could have reached the rocks, but the weight of gold strapped to their bodies dragged them down. One American paper, when describing the scenes at the wreck site said:

> A scene of confusion and terror presented itself, the horror of which can better be imagined than described. Here were the wife and husband bidding each other a last farewell, the frantic mother clasping her infant to her bosom as if death itself should not separate them; while some few who had relatives on board were endeavouring to secure what money they had, by fastening it to their bodies, but which alas proved the means of their destruction; for that which they vainly thought would secure to them a comfortable home in the fertile lands of the far "West" changed their destination to an eternal home in death. On attempting to swim to the land the weight of the money sank them to the bottom. (September 3, 1840, issue of the New York newspaper *New Era*).

While some passengers and crew were clinging to the

THE PUBLIC LEDGER

The Public Ledger.

JOHN'S, TUESDAY, August 18, 1840.

ANCHOLY SHIPWRECK.— We have the painful announce the loss of the American Brig *Flo-* of Boston, of the burthen of about 200 tons, Rose, on her passage from Rotterdam to New with passengers. The lamentable occurrence lace on the morning of Sunday the 9th instant one mile to the westward of Cape Race

WELLINGTON's speech, the developement of a of conduct on the part of Mr. Governor THOMSON, which we cannot but look upon genuous and discreditable in the extreme. her Majesty's Government is entitled to any the odium of the affair is not for us to say as likely as not.

The noble Duke observed —

He had stated to their lordships on a former effect produced in the Legislature of Upper Canad

The Newfoundland paper carries the lamentable and strange story of the *Florence*.

65

doomed ship, Captain Rose and another man reached shore with a rope. Thus, through his efforts and a line to the shore, all the crew except the second mate and thirty passengers survived; nearly fifty were lost. One man who found himself on shore was Philip Meisenheimer. His wife and five children drowned. Others were in a like situation- a father lost or a mother, children perished and, in some cases, entire families.

It is likely Captain Rose knew of Cape Race, but had little knowledge of the lay of the land or of any towns in the area. The 37 survivors had been cast upon a foreign shore without a morsel of food, with only the clothes on their backs. Some were in their bare feet.

No one in the area or in any of the small settlements near Cape Race were aware a catastrophe had taken place. Fortunately, it was August. Weather was warm, berries and brook water were plentiful. The rag-tag group walked northward, following narrow trails that skirted the long in draughts, crevices and cliffs. For five days and nights they struggled along, over barren hills, into valleys, over bogs and through thick underbrush, but saw no sign of civilization until they reached the fishing village of Renews.

Local papers of August 1840 run an ad to solicit aid and relief for the survivors of the brig *Florence*.

There the people took them in for several days, clothed and fed them. Eventually Alan Goodridge and Sons' business in Renews provided a ship and they sailed to St. John's. Again charity and goodwill saw them through. A committee, the *Florence* Subscription List, was formed to raise money and to solicit clothes. The Ladies of Dorcas Society and the St. John's Chamber of Commerce also helped provide for the castaways.

In time the committee chartered a ship to take the thirty-seven survivors to New York. Philip Meisenheimer re-married, but again lost his wife and two daughters (perhaps through natural causes). He married a third time and this union produced seven sons. Today the descendants of the Meisenheimers are to be found all over the United States. In the summer of 2003 they got together for a family reunion where the stories of the survivor of the *Florence* disaster in 1840 were re-told. The only indication that Philip had been shipwrecked was found in a single page deposition or attestation kept in a family Bible, stating the name of the brig, the captain and the names and ages of his family lost off Cape Race.

In those early years of westward movements and settlement, few records of immigrant voyages were kept and an accurate list of passengers on *Florence* is probably non-existent. But another family is known: Gertrude and Johannes Pieter (Peter) Adrian, their two sons Michael and Stephen were from Klingenberg, Bavaria. These four also survived the wreck, but a relative aunt "pulled her skirts over her head" and jumped in panic to certain death.

According to family sources, the Adrians arrived in New York penniless. However, Michael, age 13 at the time of the shipwreck, reversed his fortunes. Eventually he became a landowner in New York, founded the German Exchange Bank which later merged with and became a branch of the First National City Bank of New York. Michael Adrian had six children whose progeny are now scattered across the United States and abroad.

Lashed to the Masts

Date: *11,1870*
Location: *Between Channel and Nova Scotia*
Fatalities: *4*
Remarks: *Three Crew Survive Off Nova Scotia*

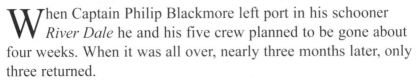

When Captain Philip Blackmore left port in his schooner *River Dale* he and his five crew planned to be gone about four weeks. When it was all over, nearly three months later, only three returned.

Philip Blackmore, his brother Tim, and Ben Buffett belonged to Channel. Three other men with him on *River Dale* hailed from Little River - Angus D. McIsaac, Angus McLean and Dan McDonald. Dan, perhaps because of his stature, was often referred to as "Big" Dan. Philip Blackmore owned the schooner and in the fall of the year, he and his men left for the Labrador on a herring fishing trip.

Little River is today St. Andrew's, a farming community situated at the mouth of the Little Codroy River about 25 kilometers north of Channel-Port aux Basques. St. Andrew's was named for the patron saint of Scotland, as some early settlers were highland Scots who emigrated to the fertile river valley from Cape Breton Island in the nineteenth century. Although most of pioneers - McNeills, McIsaacs, McDonalds, Aucoins (O'Quinns), LeBlancs, Doyles and Tompkins - were farmers, some pursued the fishery in the fall. By 1874, about the time of our story, there were 147 people living in St. Andrew's; today the population stands at a little over two hundred.

Captain Blackmore and his crew had a good trip; herring was plentiful and late in October *River Dale* again docked at Channel. There the schooner loaded 350 quintals of dried cod as consigned by a Nova Scotian merchant named Savage. He joined the ship as a passenger to Halifax.

All went well until they were well along the Nova Scotian coast when a typical, but violent fall storm came on. In those early days of all-sail, there were no long range weather forecasts, nor was there any method or means - except intuitive knowledge of mariners - available to predict sudden and heavy gales. Caught out in the treacherous Atlantic in the height of the storm, Philip Blackmore did the best he could, ordering the crew to put the sails under double reef, battening down the hatches and lashing down any moveable objects on deck.

In a short time seas became like liquid mountains. One tremendous wave struck the schooner broadside and threw it down on beam ends - with sails parallel or nearly so to the water. In this position it stayed for seemingly minutes. Captain Blackmore and Buffett were washed overboard and the crew was helpless to save them. Their two friends and workmates were never seen again. The survivors could only cling to any available ropes and hope the schooner would right itself.

Although the remaining crew on deck didn't know it at the time, passenger Savage in the cabin below deck had drowned when the cabin filled with water. In the force of heavy seas, both masts broke off near the deck and this helped *River Dale* become more stabilized. Slowly it came upright to a near even keel, but the ship was waterlogged and doomed to drift at the whims of wind and wave.

The four remaining men - Tim Blackmore, McIsaac, McLean and Big Dan - lashed themselves to the stumps of the masts and prayed they would not wash off the deck which now had white water breaking over it constantly. In this position they stayed for three days and nights with no food or drinking water and with spray or waves washing over their heads.

On the second day Angus McLean died from exposure. His comrades had no choice but cut him clear of the ropes and let his body drift to sea. On the third day the weather abated; skies cleared somewhat, enough to see a sail - a ship - in the distance. Slowly the ship veered and worked its way down to the derelict *River Dale* and its human cargo of three half-delirious men.

It proved to be an American schooner en route to Nova Scotia. The survivors were treated as well as they could be and were eventually landed in Halifax. At that time there was no steam connection between Halifax and Newfoundland's west coast; so the three survivors had to find a way home as best they could.

By hitching a ride or working a passage on small boats, they reached the Gut of Canso. By now it was nearly winter; thus few schooners to Newfoundland frequented Canso. The stranded seamen of Cape Breton's Scottish descent had relatives and friends on the west side of Cape Breton. From Canso they walked to Broad Cove near Inverness and there stayed with friends.

Dan McDonald remained in Cape Breton all winter. Angus McIsaac and Tim Blackmore walked to North Sydney, over 50 miles away and found a passage to Channel by a Newfoundland schooner. Blackmore was home; Angus McIsaac reached St. Andrew's a few days before Christmas - he had been gone nearly three months. Angus often told this story to his brother and related that time meant little when he was grateful he had escaped with his life aboard the wreck of the schooner *River Dale*.

In the Middle of Nowhere with No Food

Date: *09,1893*
Location: *On the Offshore Banks*
Fatalities: *None*
Remarks: *Two Fishermen*
               Survive an Ordeal

What hardships our forefathers and pioneers of the sea endured to put bread on the table. And perhaps the toughest, most treacherous occupation in the era of the all-sail vessels was the hook and line dory fishing on the offshore banks. When the breadwinners went to sea there was no way to predict how or when they would get back home, if at all. Death by drowning or exposure in banking schooners and the dory seemed so common-

Bonavista in a more recent era. A trap skiff, probably Johnny Russell's *Jennie R*, enters the harbour. In the background are the Ryan premises three great stores - Fish Store, Number One and the Shop.

place between 1880s and 1950s that often it went unreported in the daily papers.

This was certainly the case for two Bonavista fishermen in mid-September1893. Frederick Abbott and Job Porter (a name more commonly associated with a nearby town of Elliston) left Bonavista in the fall that year to go to the Grand Banks. Generally Bonavista's fishermen worked the inshore fishery, but in this case the two young men joined the schooner *Poppy* out of Carbonear, bound for the banks southeast of Cape Race.

The next thing heard from them was a story from the British consul in New York. Haggard, penniless, hungry, but happy to be alive, the two had been brought into the city by the Allan steamer *State of Nebraska*. It was an all-too-common tale of being adrift on the open ocean with no food or water - a misadventure that often ravaged the men of the dory fleet.

On Monday, September 18, Abbott and Porter left the mother ship at 4 a.m. to take in the trawl lines they had set the evening before. They rowed a mile from the mother ship *Poppy*. In two or three hours they hoped to be back, pronging their fish over the side of the schooner.

But the old nemesis, fog, had other plans. In the grey shroud they missed their way, failed to find the buoy to which their lines were attached and they lost their bearings or direction. When the fog lifted somewhat there was no sign of the schooner.

Then started an odyssey of five days of no rest, no place to sleep - and not so much as a biscuit to eat and not a drop of fresh water. For days they drifted at the mercy of the sea, not knowing if they were drifting toward land or to sea, or into the track of steamers or to some remote spot in the ocean.

To make matters worse, the constant pounding of waves opened seams in the dory and water trickled in slowly at first and more generously at the end. They had to bail water day and night. They were all alone until Thursday when they saw a large steamer hustling over the eastern ocean. Best of all it was bearing down in their direction.

Weak, hungry and dehydrated, they struggled to their feet, waved their caps and coats and shouted. The steamer plunged past them within a few cable lengths. It passed so near, the bobbing dory was almost swamped in the steamer's wake. It was so close that Abbott and Porter could see the crew or passengers upon its decks, crowding along the rail.

No one seemed to take any notice of the stray dory. The two toilers of the sea were again alone - this time more than hungry, thirsty and tired. They were disgusted and in utmost despair.

But there was one item in their favor: the sea was merciful, the waters were smooth and the winds light. Yet they barely had enough strength to keep the boat above water. They sat there almost in shock, bailing each in his turn. To keep their spirits up, sometimes they told stories of the sea, or they talked of boyhood days - climbing the cliffs at Canaille, walking the paths at Mockbegger, or trouting in Bayly's Cove Pond or Trinity Pond. It became a constant struggle to keep up spirits and to avoid going to sleep. For both to fall asleep at the same time would have been tempting death.

On the evening of September 21 another large steamer came along. It was almost dark when the lights of an ocean liner went past. Although they cried for help, their puny voices were lost in the roar of rushing waters.

On Friday afternoon, salvation! The S.S. *City of Nebraska* steamed by on a course to New York. Abbott and Porter waved their signals of distress and rowed as fast as their feeble strength would allow toward the vessel. *City of Nebraska* stopped its engines and waited as the dory came alongside.

Both fishermen were overcome, dropped their oars and they fell exhausted in the bottom of the dory. A seaman went down the accommodation ladder of the steamer and put ropes around the waists of the insensible men. Carefully and slowly they were hoisted on deck.

Aboard the steamer they were revived by a hot toddy and broth, but it was several days before they could eat solid food. They had no idea how far they had drifted.

When *City of Nebraska* picked them up, they were in latitude 47.58, longitude 71 and many miles from the fishing grounds of Newfoundland schooners. In New York the British Consul wired St. John's and Bonavista to let loved ones know they were rescued and made arrangements for transportation to Newfoundland.

Chapter 4
Foreign Lands and Ships

One of the first sea stories in which I learned of Newfoundland seamen struggling to survive on a "foreign" schooner wrecked on a distant shore was in the tale of the *Monclair*. While carrying lumber to
the United States in March 1927, the Nova Scotian tern stranded at
Nauset Beach, Massachusetts. Two survivors were Nathan Baggs of
Cape LaHune and Garland Short, Bonavista. Four others, including
two other Newfoundlanders, William Stewart and George Caines of
Burgeo, perished.

Over the years I subsequently located other interesting (to me
at least) tales of Newfoundland seamen standing before the mast on
ships from other provinces and countries. In the course of research
for this book, I was intrigued by the many names of our seamen who
were listed on the roster of foreign ships.

Newfoundland and Labrador mariners were hired as captains,
seamen, deck hands, cooks on ships all over the world. In this they
are not unique for the same could be said for mariners of all seafaring nations. But in common they all had the capriciousness of the sea
and the inevitable shipwreck as a factor in their lives. Plus they all
had loved ones somewhere concerned over their welfare.

The Nova Scotian songwriter in "Farewell to Nova Scotia" -
a song considered an anthem to Nova Scotian sailors and to seamen
all across the eastern seaboard - wonders if anyone thinks about him
during an ocean storm: "When I am far away on the briny ocean
tossed,
Will you ever heave a sigh and a wish for me?"

No doubt if I had access and opportunity to study archival
newspapers and material from lands beyond the sea, I would have
encountered many more of our island seamen on foreign ships.
These nine tales then are just a fraction of those that could be told.

In the Face of Death off the Labrador

Date:	*08,1910*
Location:	*off Labrador*
Fatalities:	*None*
Remarks:	*Four Days of Hardship in a Dory*

They faced death. They knew it. To make it easier and to cheer each other up, the two men sang every old song and hymn they knew. After four days of total isolation and exposure, they knew time was up; both men resigned themselves to perish on the high seas.

Samuel Cole was older than his nephew Nicholas Cole, but both were dory mates fishing off Labrador in August 1910. Both were from Conception Bay, Newfoundland. Although the exact town where they were born is not recorded, Victoria, an inland community near Carbonear, has a great concentration of Coles, but it is likely they belonged to one of the many seaside fishing towns of Conception Bay. However, at the time of their death-defying experience, they were employed on a ship out of Massachusetts. The story they told after rescue was one of hardship and determination to survive.

The schooner *Essex*, owned and operated out of Gloucester, Massachusetts, and commanded by Captain Michael Wise, sought halibut in Arctic waters east of Labrador. On July 23, 1910, the two Coles who were employed on *Essex*, were hauling their trawls when an unexpected gale separated them from their vessel. Within a hour darkness came and by daylight the next morning the schooner was nowhere in sight.

Both men knew the situation was most alarming for several reasons: a storm was raging and they were far from the track of shipping. More serious the fact that they had no food aboard the dory and little water. Help would have to come within five or six days or they would perish.

On the first night astray, the younger Cole felt it was useless to fight - odds were stacked too much against them. The elder Cole talked to him at length and boosted his spirits some-what. They sang church hymns, children's nonsense songs and the old ballads and folk songs passed down through the years.

Fortunately the small craft was equipped with a sail and compass. When the wind swung around and moderated, it was toward land - about one hundred twenty-five miles away they reckoned.

The Western St...

BAY OF ISLANDS, NEWFOUNDLAND, WEDNESDAY, AUGUST 24, 1910.

A GOOD ADVERTISING MEDIUM

Newspaper Published In Western Newfoundland,

Sang Ballads In Face Of Death

Reached Land After Four Days in Their Dory

WITHOUT FOOD

Young Nicholas Cole began to suffer from hunger and wanted to eat the raw halibut in the dory, but his Uncle Sam stopped him with the words, "Eating raw fish when one is starving will drive you crazy." Sam Cole had heard stories of men driven to delirium with the salt that would con-taminate the raw food.

For four days they drifted toward land without proper nourishment and, since they were in the iceberg lanes, they had to maintain a constant vigilance. Once Nicholas Cole became hard-ened to the privations, he became tougher and helped keep the dory on course toward land. As time went on both men did not feel the pangs of hunger as much, but knew their bodies were weaker.

Finally on the fourth day adrift, they saw the dim, indis-tinct haze of land. But by now the wind had shifted again, off the land and full in their face. Their dory, like all dories had a flat bottom and, while stable, did not sail well to the windward. Both castaways manned the oars fearful they would be again blown to sea. Against the wind, they rowed all day and covered about five miles.

As night fell they saw the lights of another craft. It seemed to be lying to or stopped under the lee of Ironbound Island, near the Labrador coast. It proved to be, as they discovered later, a Newfoundland schooner, but referred to as a "green" fisherman.

The operator kept its fish fresh or green under much salt until the voyage was over.

Much to the surprise of those on the Newfoundland schooner (whose name is not given) two weak and lost souls rowed up to the side and had to be helped aboard. Nicholas and Sam Cole were so feeble from cramped conditions and lack of nourishment, they could scarcely stand on their feet.

The Newfoundland skipper did everything he could to help them: whatever he had he gave freely, hard biscuits soaked in tea, and gave up his berth to them. He woke them every three hours to administer more small portions of food until they had recovered enough to be able to eat as much as they wanted without danger.

After several days aboard the schooner, the government steamer *Susu*, commanded by Captain Winsor, came to the Labrador coast on its regular run and took the men aboard. They were landed at St. John's and the United States consulate sent them to their homes in Massachusetts.

Lifeboat Missing

Date:	*03, 1920*
Location:	*On the Grand Banks*
Fatalities:	*8*
Remarks:	*Lifeboat from a Sunken Trawler Unreported*

In the 1920s, some of the first Nova Scotian trawlers were making an appearance on the east coast fishing banks. Just after the Great War many schooners were replaced by trawlers and gradually the traditional fish catching methods with hook and line and the wooden banking schooners phased out.

Many early trawlers were wooden and were powered by steam engines fed by coal. Coal took up valuable space and when the ships had little aboard, they had to return to port to replenish. This was the case with the trawler *M.F.B.* which left Liverpool,

Nova Scotia, in late March 1920 for the banks. It had a successful week fishing, but Captain Kramp was bothered by a slow but persistent leak. But it didn't interfere with fishing and work must go on.

On April 3, laden with 90,000 pound of fish, it left the banks for Halifax to refill its coal bunkers. Thirty-five miles off port, the engineer reported the ship was leaking badly aft. The crew ran the pumps, but these could not cope with the inflow. After three hours sea water reached the engine room, put out the fires and *M.F.B.*, without steam power, stopped.

Kramp decided it was useless to stand by the ship and gave orders to launch the two lifeboats and the dory. Before he left *M.F.B.* at 8:30 p.m., Captain Kramp sent up flares and rockets to attract attention of any other craft which may have been in the general area. But finally the twenty crew - eight in each of the two lifeboats and four in the dory - rowed away from the sinking trawler. By now the decks were awash.

With the captain in charge of one lifeboat and the first mate, the other, the three boats kept together for several hours, but Captain Kramp reported afterward that the last he saw of the other lifeboat was at ten p.m. The second boat, in charge of first officer Turner, was well-manned with some of the best seamen on the trawler.

The plan was for the dory to keep between the two lifeboats for as long as possible, but gradually the second

Survivors of the Sinking of Trawler *M.F.B*
Captain Kramp, Holland
chief engineer Freeman Brophy, Shelburne, NS
second engineer Anthony J. Arsenault, Charlottetown
engineer P. Morreau, Quebec
second officer R. Suddaby, Hull, England
seaman John Burton, Bay St. Lawrence, NS
seaman, Joseph Kay, St. Pierre
seaman, R.E. ?, Canso, NS
seaman, William O'Brien, St. Peter's, NS
fireman A. Domely, Chester, NS
cook Wilson Mosher, Bristol, England
assistant cook N. H. Hannaberry, ?

lifeboat dropped behind. Occasionally at night the boats communicated with each other by flares.

As is the age-old story with the treacherous sea, the wind came up at night accompanied by rain squalls which changed to heavy cold rain, making everyone miserable. Neither the captain nor his bosun had any oil clothes and the rain saturated them to the skin for the eight hour row.

After twelve p.m. those in the lifeboat and the dory saw a steamer's lights. When the lights reappeared, the steamer had changed position. Kramp reasoned it had located something on the ocean, possibly the second lifeboat and was looking around for other lifeboats.

At four a.m. it was impossible for the shipwrecked crew to make any further progress in the wind and a drag, or temporary anchor, was put out to slow or stop the boat. At this point the four seamen in the dory transferred to the larger lifeboat. There was still no sign of the missing lifeboat and Captain Kramp grew more and more uneasy.

At daylight they resumed rowing, saw land at 11:30 and reached it soon after. By April 8 the other lifeboat still had not shown up. Kramp held off on uttering the words, "Missing, presumed lost" and refused to believe the worst had happened. "The boat was staunch," he said, "similar to the one I was in and had experienced seamen aboard."

It was not likely they were still drifting on the Atlantic, but could have been picked up by a steamer or schooner, perhaps they landed in some remote point along the shore. Yet there was the possibility the lifeboat met misfortune on some rocky offshore ledge.

Newfoundland papers carried the story on April 19, with the tragic heading **Newfoundlanders Lost From N.S. Trawler**. There were two aboard that second lifeboat - Michael Drake of St. Lawrence and F. Tipple of St.

John's, although the first name of the latter is not given and most likely the last name is mis-spelled. The other six lost at sea were first mate George Turner, Hull, England; fireman T. Quinn, Isle of Man, England; firemen John Arsenault and A. Collins, both of Charlottetown, PEI and two seamen from Nova Scotia, William Morton, Liverpool, and R.D. Dollivar, Eastport.

Kramp had spent thirty years trawling out of his home country, Holland. In his opinion a wooden trawler was not strong enough to withstand the rigors of the stormy Atlantic in winter and to keep up with the demands which deep sea fishing put on it. He said, "The only ship suitable for the work is one built of steel."

He was right in that steel ships would replace the wooden vessels, but in the years ahead even some of those fell prey to the voracious Atlantic.

Fire and Collision

Date: *05,1946*
Location: *Off Nova Scotia*
Fatalities: *None*
Remarks: *Collision at Sea*

Newfoundland seamen were employed all over the maritimes, and just as often as not, were involved with misadventure at sea. On May 24, 1946, while the Charlottetown-registered *Nellie Nixon* was en route from Port au Port to Sydney, Nova Scotia, fire broke out in the schooner's bunker oil tanks. Captain Uriah Giles was fourteen miles off Flat Point, North Sydney harbour, when the blaze was discovered.

Nellie Dixon, owned by the Margaree Steamships Company of Sydney, had been built at Boston, Massachusetts, in1888. Despite its considerable age, the 60-ton schooner was in good condition.

With Giles were seaman Willard Keeping of Ramea, Don and Lucene Ryan, Baddeck, Nova Scotia, Harold Parsons, North Sydney. Also listed as crew was Thomas Corkum whose place of residence was given as Burin, Newfoundland, but may be in error as the name Corkum is not associated with Burin, rather Lunenburg, Nova Scotia.

There was little time to fight a blaze and Captain Giles shouted orders to abandon ship. Flames were leaping one hundred feet into the air by the time the ship's dory pulled away.

It was early morning and the blaze could be seen for miles. Robert Belmore, a young man from North Sydney and captain/owner of the fishing boat *Happy Girl*, saw the fire. Although Belmore knew it would cost him a day's fishing, he sailed down near the burning craft. Within an hour all were rescued and Belmore landed the crew at North Sydney.

On July 14, 1953, the Lunenburg schooner *Greenrock* was headed home from the waters off Newfoundland. Captain John Mills and his 27 crew had a good catch of fish. In the dense fog about 17 miles southwest from Whitehead, Nova Scotia, at 11:10 p.m., the American dragger *Thomas D* ran into the schooner and in a few minutes *Greenrock* went to the bottom.

One of the crew was Walter G. Pierce of Harbour Breton. In a story carried by *The Harbour Breton Coaster* on March 5, 1992, Pierce, who was interviewed by Penny Pierce, recalled:

Crew of *Greenrock*, cut down July 14, 1953

Capt. John Mills - Doctor's Cove/Belleoram
Aloysius Baker - Broad Cove/Harbour Breton
Ralph Farrell - Harbour Breton
Eric Ashford - Harbour Breton
Walter G. Pierce - Harbour Breton
Dave Skinner - Harbour Breton
George Tom Skinner - Harbour Breton
John Skinner - Harbour Breton
Richard Skinner - Harbour Breton
Sam Strickland - Harbour Breton
Richard Martin - Harbour Breton
John Joe Ridgeley - Miller's Passage
Michael Ridgeley - Miller's Passage
Tom Ridgeley - Miller's Passage
Bill T. Sheppard - Miller's Passage
Leo Snook - Miller's Passage
Clarence Bartlett - Coomb's Cove
Stephen Blagdon - Coomb's Cove
Stephen Drake - Coomb's Cove
Harold Vallis - Coomb's Cove
Alex Hillier - Brunette
Silas Hillier - Brunette
Alex Hardiman - Point Rosie
Thomas Keeping - English Harbour East
Charles Strickland - ?/Lunenburg, NS

The weather was fine and the schooner was making good time on its way to Nova Scotia. After dark, fog set in but that was no big deal. We expected to be in Lunenburg by early morning. But this did not happen. About 11 p.m. the 120-foot *Greenrock* ran into something. All hands went on deck and were shocked to see that another vessel, the *Thomas D*, had collided with us. Realizing the major damage done to *Greenrock*, the skipper decided to abandon ship.

Our ship was split fair in half by *Thomas D*, but there was no loss of life in the incident. Some shipmates escaped with only minor cuts and bruises.

All crew members were picked up by the other vessel and carried to Lunenburg and were put up in boarding houses. The crew was given clean clothes and plenty of good food to eat.

Walter, who was 17 years old at the time, did not come home right away; he and several other shipmates finished the summer voyage on another Nova Scotian schooner *Theresa E. Connor*. Zwicker and Company figured the value of *Greenrock* at $11,000. Captain Mills, a veteran and cautious captain, lost his life at sea a little over ten years later. On December 20, 1963, the coasting schooner *Mary Pauline* ran into a storm and sank near St. Pierre. Six of seven crew, including Mills, perished. Sylvester Hynes of St. Bernard's survived.

"A Slim Chance for our Lives"

Date:	*12,1926*
Location:	*Mouth of Halifax Harbour*
Fatalities:	*None*
Remarks:	*Seamen Survive a Shipwreck*

Four Newfoundland seamen and two Nova Scotians had no choice but to jump from a ship into the tossing seas and then to try to swim among the wave-lashed rocks. Drastic action indeed, but it was in preference to remain on their ship or to launch the lifeboat. To do either would mean certain death; at least by swimming they had a chance to survive.

The *South Head*, described by most seamen as a handsome schooner, had a colorful and stormy career. Its life began as *Helen Mathers* at the Shelburne Shipping Company in 1919 and was first owned by I.H. Mathers of Halifax. On a return voyage from Europe, during which it lost all sails, the vessel was driven ashore on the coast of Texas in June 1921. *Helen Mathers* remained on the beach for a year until sold to new owners in the Cayman Islands and renamed *Ella B.*

The tern was then chartered to rum runners and, in February 1925, arrived at Lunenburg, Nova Scotia, with a cargo of liquor in the hold. Four crew were jailed for alleged assault on other crew members. The schooner and owners were sued by the crew for back wages. The supercargo, in charge of the cargo, disappeared after *Ella B* arrived in port and no one showed up on behalf of the owners to claim or sell the cargo, consisting of 40,000 cases of liquor.

Not long after, another claim was made on the vessel and its cargo by the owners of the schooner *Veronica*. The latter alleged the liquor had been high-jacked or stolen on the high seas by the crew of *Ella B.* After this revelation, rumors circulated the schooner was the property of New York gangsters involved in the rum running trade.

At any rate the vessel was auctioned off at a sheriff's sale on April 25, 1925, for the sum of $10,200, with the lucky, or perhaps unlucky, new owner as Captain Samuel Shaw of Dartmouth. He renamed the schooner *South Head*. When sold - at way less than its true value - the highly-prized liquor cargo helped pay off damages done to *Veronica* for piracy on the high seas.

Snatched from the Sea: Crew of *South Head*, December 6, 1926.

Captain Stanley Shaw, Dartmouth

mate John Saunders, Halifax

cook Sydney Weymouth, Grand Bank, NL

seaman Stanley Strickland, Burgeo, NL

seaman Sandy Hatcher, Burgeo, NL

seaman Arthur Fraser, St. George's, NL

seaman Edwin Kendall, NL

Its greatest misadventure came December 6, 1926, while in command of Samuel Shaw's son, Stanley. At 6:30 a.m., while bound for Halifax in ballast from St. Pierre, *South Head* ran head-long into a full-fledged winter storm. Captain Shaw stood in south of Sandwich Point at the entrance to Halifax harbour, hoping to shelter from the storm. Finding the schooner would not tack and realizing that problem would put the schooner on the rocks, Shaw ordered out the two anchors.

The flukes could not get sufficient hold on the bottom to stop the great vessel. It gradually dragged anchors until the ship struck with a shattering blow on Sandwich Point. Captain Shaw best described what happened:

The *Halifax Evening Mail* headlines of December 6, 1926, features the wreck of two schooners: *W.C. Smith* (centre) and *South Head.* Newfoundlanders were on both ships and barely escaped with their lives.

We anchored inside Herring Cove and about midnight it started to snow. The *South Head* dragged its anchors and was driven inside the ledges. Between six and seven this morning (December 6, 1926) we realized that unless we abandoned the vessel that we would have a slim chance for our lives, as the seas were sweeping over it.

We swung the spanker boom out over the side, climbed along to the end of the boom to the ledges and reached the shore. We had a marvelous escape.

Shaw realized that even a vessel of the fine construction of the *South Head* would not last, hanging as it was on the jagged rocks and open to the buffeting of the wild seas. Every wave swept over it.

The only choice was to swing the spanker boom over the stern, drop from it, and swim to shore. The battle between human muscle and will and the pull of the surf was terrific. Once their hands and feet touched the rocks, they had to clamber over it. The local paper said,

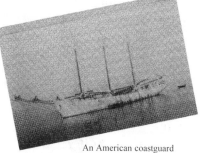

An American coastguard photo of *South Head* in the days it when it was the rum runner *Ella B*. Five Newfoundlanders survived its wreck on December 6, 1926.

> Their escape from death in the icy waters, lashed to a fury by a gale, is conceded to be miraculous. In the annals of wrecks along the shores in the vicinity of Halifax, the experiences of *South Head*'s crew stand well to the fore.

The plight of *South Head* had been seen by the life saving station at Herring Cove. Thomas Brown, coxswain of the boat crew, and his group made a brave attempt to launch the boat, but couldn't get away from the surf. Both G.S. Campbell and Company's boats, the *Sampson* and *Coalopolis* were sent to Sandwich, but could be of no assistance.

The stranded mariners were taken into Herring Cove homes. Shaw, who had received some injuries as did another seamen, lodged with Mr. Brackett.

South Head was not the only Nova Scotia schooner lost that night. At Little Port L'Herbert, the two-masted schooner *W.C. Smith*, Captain J.M. Petipas, struck a rock at the end of Johnson's Pond Beach near the village. Petipas, his son Fred Petipas of Halifax, Sam Martin, Newfoundland, Alex Williams, Halifax, and Jason Walters and Pearly Mason, both of Lunenburg, put off the dory and battled their way into the beach.

Had they remained aboard the schooner, it would have been certain death for *W.C. Smith* went to pieces off the beach. Immediately after they reached shore, the crew was taken into Steven Harding's home. The 140-ton *W.C. Smith* was built in Lunenburg in 1910 for W.C. Smith and Company. At the time of its loss it carried 650,000 laths owned by J.F. Logan of Halifax and destined for New York.

St. John's Captain Dies at the Wheel

Date:	*06, 1895*
Location:	*Off Iceland*
Fatalities:	*1*
Remarks:	*Newfoundland Captain Dies at the Wheel*

Captain Joseph Ryan was born in St. John's, but as a young man had gone to Gloucester, Massachusetts, to find work on the banking schooners. By 1895 he had risen through the ranks of fishermen and commanded the Gloucester banking schooner *A. D. Storey*. In mid-June 1895 he was off Iceland fishing for halibut.

As was the usual method of trawl fishing in those times all dory men paired up and left the schooner to bait or take fish from the hook and line trawls. Only the captain and cook would be left aboard; the cook tended his work in the galley preparing meals, the captain stood to the wheel, keeping his vessel to the wind and near the ten or twelve dories scattered around the mother ship.

When the dory men left an hour or so before, the captain seemed to be in good health. The vessel was under way and a strong breeze had come up. The captain, who was at the wheel, collapsed at his work and, within a moment, passed away.

Somehow, the cook realized there was a problem and came on deck. With great difficulty, for he was cross-handed and unfamiliar with the tending of sail, he managed to keep the vessel in the vicinity of the dories. When he saw his chance he ran a signal flag up the rigging to signal to the men there was trouble. They came on board; the mate took charge and sailed *A.D. Storey* into a town in Iceland where the remains of Captain Ryan were landed. Ryan, a seasoned skipper who had made many voyages to the Arctic regions for halibut, left a wife and two children in Gloucester.

Schooner *Fortuna*,
Ill-Fortune for Newfoundland

Date:	*01, 1896*
Location:	*Off Cape Cod*
Fatalities:	*9*
Remarks:	*Banking Schooner Cut Down on the Fishing Grounds*

Often the notices of disaster and death at sea are brief. One can read, in a shipping casualty list, the entry (for December 25, 1905) "*Robert S. Besnard* of Parrsboro, struck by a water spout, eastern coast of North America." This terse entry leaves many unanswered questions: Where there survivors? What was their version of the rare event? A water spout? How many other ships have survived that kind of encounter? Another shipping note reads, "November 1911, Lunenburg-built *Arkansas*, Missing in the Atlantic (6 crew members lost). " Who were they? How and where did the final plunge of the ship take place?

A similar brief statement appears in *The Harbour Grace Standard* for January 31, 1896: Three Newfoundlanders lost in the sinking of Gloucester "Fortuna" on January 13, 1896 - Robert Childs, single, age 28; John Clarke; and William Tobin, single, age 30. Ship sunk by "Barnstable."

Further delving reveals nothing, at least as far as this searcher is concerned and there are more questions raised than answered. Neither Clarke's martial status or age is given. It must have been a collision at sea. Did any Newfoundlanders survive? Did anyone?

It may be only a searcher's good luck, but the secret of the fate of the Gloucester banker *Fortuna* appeared in Gordon Thomas' book *Fast and Able*. Yet his book doesn't list any victims or survivors. Again one has to combine the two accounts.

Fortuna, under Captain Greenlaw, did well on the fishing grounds. It was close to home when it met its fate. On January 13, 1896, while running off before the wind on a clear moonless night, *Fortuna* was rammed by the fruit steamer *Barnstable*, six miles off Cape Cod. The only men on the schooner's deck at the time were Captain Greenlaw at the wheel and the man who stood watch and a lookout up forward.

The lookout on the steamer could not see the schooner's lights as they were obscured by the sails. *Fortuna* was struck amidship and the steamer's bow sliced through the schooner, almost severing it in two pieces. The steel prow of the great ship blocked the forecastle companionway, preventing the men trapped below from escaping. Nine men went to their deaths. Cook Arthur Nunan helped save several lives by opening the bulkhead into the forehold.

Barnstable's captain kept the prow of the steamer into the hole made into *Fortuna* and slowly forced the schooner ahead. By doing this, the 14 survivors were able to climb the bow of the steamer to safety. The last man had hardly reached the deck of the steamer when *Fortuna* went to the bottom. Three of those who went down with the ship were the Newfoundland fishermen Childs, Clarke and Tobin.

Chasing the *Potomac*

U. S. Naval Tug Potomac in the Ice
(Newspaper sketch)

Date: 03, 1914
Location: West Coast
Fatalities: None
Remarks: American Vessel
              "Potomac" in Ice

In the first decades of the twentieth century, 1900-1920, American schooners were still frequenting Newfoundland's west coast in great numbers. They were chiefly interested in herring - frozen for bait necessary to pursue the great cod fishery off Canada and New England, or pickled or cured herring for consumption. This lucrative trade occurred chiefly in the winter months when the herring could be frozen by Newfoundland suppliers.

To protect and aid its schooners - which often became stuck in winter ice floes should the vessels delay leaving or if fall frost came early - the American govern- ment sent its small naval ships to the coast. In February 1914, the U.S. Naval Tug *Potomac* ran into trouble itself while attempting to free American schooners off Bonne Bay.

Around February 9, *Potomac* was caught in the floes in Bonne Bay Bight, about 5 miles north northwest of Lobster Head Light. The crew, feeling there was little chance of getting free, abandoned the tug. The 20 ton of coal and provisions aboard could last fifteen days, but *Potomac*'s captain figured the ship would be stuck in ice for several weeks beyond that.

On February 11, *Potomac*'s first officer arrived in Woody Point to ask locals to carry provisions out to the ship. Subsequently a group of men and horses delivered good and supplies to Rocky Harbour. By that time ice, pushed in by a heavy northwest wind, was jammed solid on the land. If the wind changed there was a possibility *Potomac* could be freed, but the chances were slim.

One local mariner, Captain Coleman who was well versed in ice and wind conditions on the West Coast, was asked about a similar incident in the winter of 1903. He was one of the men who boarded the ice-bound schooner *A. M. Nicholson* after it had been abandoned by its crew.

On February 14, 1903, Coleman and three other men walked offshore for several miles from Bonne Bay and boarded the *Nicholson*. But it was the last day of May before the schooner became free from the ice. During all that time the ice kept moving up and down the west coast with a tendency to drift northward.

Coleman claimed the current had a greater control than the wind over ice movement.

Potomac was now officially abandoned; its propeller had fallen off in the crush of ice. By the time the crew reached land at Lobster Head, one of the crew had his feet frozen while walking to land. By February 18 the tug drifted north and had been sighted north of Parsons Pond - its crew however proceeded on south to the Bay of Islands and Curling.

But an abandoned ship off Newfoundland is very attractive to would-be salvagers. One account coming into Curling stated:

> Report reaches here that the *Potomac* had been looted and considerable damage done to her woodwork. If such be the case, it is to very much regretted, for parties guilty are liable for prosecution.

By early March, when word came down *Potomac* had been sighted off Spirity Cove, Port Saunders, certain groups of salvagers made plans to reach this valuable prize.

Salvage Group Which Reached *Potomac* mid-March 1914	
John LeMoine	William LeMoine
Absalom Wells	Alphonse DeLaroche
John Pennell	James O'Rourke

The American Consular, O.C. Gould, stationed in Bay of Islands, contracted Captain John Gillam of Channel to fit out his schooner *Bessie Jennox* to load coal and proceed to *Potomac* as soon as ice and weather conditions improved. Another group, H. Carter and his party, left from Cow Head and were thought to have reached the ship by walking over the ice.

Another group, led by John LeMoine, left Curling to walk north, carrying two large hand pumps. They hoped to pump out the ship; deemed necessary before getting the ship's steam engines into operation.

LeMoine's group left Curling March 15 with the two iron pumps, weighing about 200 pounds. After three weeks of hard travel they reached Bonne Bay on the 17th, proceeded to Sally's Cove which they reached on the 19th. Weather held them up for a day. They walked on to Cow Head, reaching there at 4 in the evening, all the while walking through a fierce snow storm. Thoughts that the American tug could drift across the Straits and beyond help gave the salvagers a strong sense of urgency.

At Cow Head, they received news *Potomac* had driven off to about three miles west of Spirity Cove. In harsh weather they traveled on, reaching Portland Creek on March 21 and the next day arriving at Spirity Cove, a now-abandoned community on the southern approaches to Ingornachoix Bay. *Potomac* was drifting towards the Strait of Belle Isle and was last seen off Flat Island in St. John Bay.

LeMoine and his men pushed on to Port au Choix and reached there March 25. *Potomac* was off the Eastern Twins and they walked over the ice the vessel. Att 1:10 p.m. they finally boarded their elusive goal; to their disappointment Carter's group was already on board with the engines in working order.

John LeMoine stayed aboard. The rest of his group went

to Ferrole, went to Port au Choix the next day and then left to walk back to Curling. LeMoine sent a telegram back to Curling to say *Potomac* was not leaking, the engines were working well and

Curling in the era of sailing vessels. In the background (with its bowsprit near the horse's head) is a schooner with a cutwater stem. People enjoy a sleigh ride on the frozen harbour.

there was ten ton of coal aboard. Reports of looting had been exaggerated for the American naval tug was in good condition.

Potomac was eventually freed from the ice in May and returned to service after repairs.

Collision off Prince Edward Island

Date: *05, 1962*
Location: *Off P.E.I.*
Fatalities: *None*
Remarks: *Wreck of the Schooner "C.A. Roland"*

In the late 1950s and early 1960s, the coasting schooner trade was still in full swing. The wooden schooner, out of vogue for the salt cod industry in most parts of Newfoundland, brought goods to coastal Newfoundland. The term "coasting trade" meant coal from Sydney, flour and sugar from Sydney and Halifax, livestock and vegetables, mostly potatoes from Prince Edward Island.

C.A. Roland before repairs. Shortly after Chessel Irving of Murray Harbour, PEI, purchased the coaster. Over the years several Newfoundland seamen found work on this vessel: Tom Evans, Mose Ambrose; Stan Rose and Theo Hatcher, Rose Blanche; Phil and Joe Fiander, English Harbour West and Jim Douglas, Brunette Island.

With the completion of the Trans Canada Highway across Newfoundland in 1965 and with improvements to branch roads leading out to the smaller, more isolated villages, the trucking industry supplanted the coasting schooner.

In May 1962 *C. A. Roland*, built 32 years before, was a workhorse in the coasting trade, old but serviceable. At one period it was owned by Percy White, Royal White and Dan Horton who all lived in the Murray Harbour area. Crilly M. Lea and Chessel Irving of Murray Harbor figured the *Roland*, as it was affectionately known, was still serviceable although it needed extensive repair work and around 1958 purchased the schooner for the coasting trade.

By May 18 the *Roland* was fully loaded with potatoes and turnip destined for Grand Bank, Newfoundland. Captain Clyde Keeping of English Harbour West had a crew of Newfoundland seamen with him.

Early the next morning, Saturday, it left Murray Harbour and was making its way through fog. Some eight miles southeast of East Point Light, PEI, some of the crew saw lights of a much larger ship coming through the fog. "I threw the engines into reverse," said Captain Keeping, "and tried to bring us about but it was too late."

Two men were asleep in the bow of the 92-foot schooner. Seaman James Bishop, age 57, and Thomas Osborne, 55, managed to scramble up on deck and into the dory the others had freed from the lashings. Keeping recalled:

> The ship hit us forward and shaved about seven feet off the bow. All we had to do was put the dories over the side and scramble into them before *C. A. Roland* sank. My radar was not working before the collision.

In thirty minutes, the schooner nodded its final farewell and slipped to the bottom. The crew rowed away from the vessel which a few minutes before was their home on the sea. The minesweeper located the dory and moved cautiously over to it. Captain Keeping saw it was the American minesweeper identified only as *U.S. 292*.

Keeping asked what the minesweeper was doing in Canadian waters and so close to land. It turned out that the ship had been recently built at a Great Lakes port and was on its way to Boston, via the waters off Prince Edward Island. *U.S. 292* received superficial damage and, after dropping the crew off at Port Hawksbury, continued on to Boston. The crew found transportation to North Sydney and made their way home on the coastal boat.

Crew of *C.A. Roland* May 19, 1962

Capt. Clyde Keeping, English Harbour West, NL
Thomas Osbourne, English Harbour West, NL
James Bishop, English Harbour West, NL
second engineer Philip Power, English Harbour West, NL
William Fizzard, English Harbour West, NL
chief engineer Owen Hickey, Curling

Shipwreck was nothing new for Phil Power for this was his third in his young life. He had been on the schooner *Alcala* with Captain Frank Poole of Belleoram when it struck the Dog Ribs Ledge off Battle Harbour, Labrador, on August 1, 1958. Less than four months later he found employment on the Clifford Shirley and Sons coaster *Philip Wayne* as engineer. While en route from PEI to Newfoundland on November 12, 1958, it ran into a storm.

Rather than attempt a Gulf of St. Lawrence crossing Captain Reuben Evans of English Harbour West decided to shelter in Cheticamp harbour. Evans had never been in Cheticamp before and somehow missed the navigational lights. *Philip Wayne* stranded on the southeast side, never to be refloated. Engineer Power then found employment on the schooner *Shirley Ann W*, owned by Royal White of Murray Harbour.

C.A. Roland's cargo and hull was fully insured by a Charlottetown insurance firm. Estimates put the replacement cost at about $100,000.00, a prohibitive amount in an era when the coasting trade was drawing to a close and work for such schooners was getting harder and harder to find.

C.A. Roland (above, left) at the Murray Harbour premises where it would load produce for Newfoundland. When it was cut down and sunk in May 1962, all six Newfoundland seamen aboard survived. Photo courtesy Tammy MacLeod and Chessel Irving, PEI

Last Seen at Bell Island

Date: 11,1933
Location: The Atlantic
Fatalities: 27
Remarks: Newfoundlander Aboard Ship Which Disappears
             in the Atlantic

The S.S. *Saxilby*'s last port of call was Bell Island, Conception Bay, where it loaded ore from the iron mine, but after it left Newfoundland waters in early November1933, the steamer disappeared. Often referred to as a "barter" steamer, the 346-foot long *Saxilby* steamed to Port Talbot, Wales, to trade the ore for Welsh coal. November storms respect no ship regardless of size or mission and soon *Saxilby* ploughed headlong into a mid-Atlantic storm.

Saxilby, with six cemented bulkheads and a cellular double bottom, was well-designed for Atlantic trade. Launched in 1914 from Ropner & Sons yards, the 3630-ton steamer was equipped with wireless communications, a direction finder and had triple expansion engines. But despite its construction and navigational aids it sent out a SOS on November 15, requesting immediate assistance. Its position was then about 400 miles off Valentin, Ireland. The next message said the 27 crew was abandoning ship and trying to launch the lifeboats.

Cunard liner *Berengaria*, the British freighter *Manchester Regiment* and the Dutch steamer *Boschdjk*, which were closest to the reported co-ordinates, steamed to the area, keeping a vigilant lookout for lifeboats. By one a.m. November 16 *Berengaria* was in the last reported position of the troubled steamer, but found nothing. Others ships reached the vicinity to search. Two days later shipping authorities reported little hope remained

SAXILBY

Photo of *Saxilby* from Hubert Hall

95

that any crew had survived. No small boat could have weathered an Atlantic hurricane and two or three days of mountainous seas.

No trace was ever found of the boats or *Saxilby*'s wreckage and no official crew list appeared in Newfoundland papers. The family of sailor Joseph O'Kane, a seaman on *Saxilby*, tell an interesting tale of the sea. He put a message in a cocoa tin saying good-by to his family. It washed up on his hometown beach of Aberavon, Wales, three years later.

Another of *Saxilby*'s crew was twenty-seven year old George Tilley. He was born on the Battery in St. John's, the son of George Tilley. He had two brothers, John and Edward of St. John's, and a brother and two sisters living in the United States.

THE DAILY NEWS

ST. JOHN'S, NEWFOUNDLAND, THURSDAY, NOVEMBER 16, 1933

Price Two Cents

No. 257

oal Barter Steamer Sinks in Storm

! Saxilby Founders In Mid Atlantic

HENDERSON MERELY THREATENED RESIGN

Bell Island Ore Carrier With 6,000 Tons Iron Ore Abandoned by Crew of 27 Who Take to Boats

Chapter 5
Disappearances and Tragedy

In a way this section became the most difficult to write. When a ship disappears from the ken of human kind, what is there to say? The port it last left? the crew, if known? the size and destination of the ship? With no survivors, no one to tell the tale, there may be precious little to record. No one knows the hour of the fatal plunge, the circumstances that caused it, nor can anyone tell in words the hardship, the pain, the anguish suffered by a crew facing eternity or, for that matter, the family left to wait and hope. The last story in the previous chapter - the disappearance of the S.S. *Saxilby* - illustrates an irksome lack of specifics around a lost ship.

Several years ago I read the minute book of a local fraternal organization. In the years of 1911 and 1912, the minutes reflected the sadness surrounding the loss of two ships from Grand Bank. In one instance, the schooner *Dorothy Louise* was long overdue and presumed lost with crew. The captain was a brother in the lodge. The recorder of the minutes wrote that the lodge master announced to the membership present, "Things are looking dark for the *Dorothy Louise*." The ship was never heard of again, lost somewhere in the Atlantic between Portugal and Newfoundland.

Good reader, you will notice in this section that the story with a great number of losses - 13 in the "Six Brothers Leshane" - has the least information. Despite a careful search of papers of the time very little could be found. It was only through the gravestone inscription and the anecdotal information from William Pellerin, a descendant of one of the victims, that I was able to find anything at all to tell.

On the other hand, the very first story "King's Cove Mysteries" is much longer. Why? It seems as if someone remembered the bits and pieces of stories of the ship *Edward* prior to its leaving St. John's. This, coupled with information about the McGrath involvement, fleshed out the tale a little more. But that's the way it is when you write a sea story - you go with what you have.

This 'going with what you have' has a two-fold effect: it often results in others remembering and offering other information (too late of course to be included in this book). But the most important effect is that the story is finally written on paper, as accurately as circumstances permit, for all to read.

So, if you research your ancestors and their ships or intend to write about them, don't fret about brevity; it all fits into a wide mosaic - threads which help make the whole more meaningful.

King's Cove Mysteries

Date: *10,1828*
Location: *Between King's Cove*
               and St. John's
Fatalities: *Several*
Remarks: *King's Cove Ships*
               Lost with Crew

It seems as if some Newfoundland towns, perhaps because of their proximity to the fishing grounds or because it sends a fleet of ships down to the sea, have more than a fair share of sea mysteries and tragedy. King's Cove, located in Blackhead Bay and a few kilometres southwest of Bonavista, is one such community.

In the fall of 1828 the schooner *Agnes* was chartered at St. John's to sail to King's Cove and there to load fish for the foreign market. Thomas McGrath, who was in St. John's at the time, was engaged as a pilot to help navigate the vessel to King's Cove. En route a rigging block or tackle broke on the main mast and the mainsail had to be lowered. It was near dusk and before repairs were made, night came on bringing with it a blinding snow storm and north west hurricane which lasted several days.

According to William Maguire of Groton, Massachusetts, a direct descendant of Captain Thomas McGrath and King's Cove seaman, James Flynn, the *Agnes* never reached King's Cove. During the winter of 1828-9 another vessel sailed into Trinity and reported finding the *Agnes* in mid-ocean with its spars cut away and no crew on board.

One can only imagine the hardship and trauma this tale caused. There was no further news of the ship until the following May when Thomas McGrath arrived in King's Cove and he told what had happened. As he and his crew neared the town, a north west gale pushed them well off to sea. The ballast shifted, and the *Agnes* was thrown on its beam ends, or on its side with masts and sails parallel or near-parallel with the water.

McGrath, an experienced sea captain, knew what to do in such circumstances; he ordered the spars cut away and slowly the vessel regained an even keel. But now *Agnes* leaked and for seventeen days the crew laboured day and night to keep the water out and to keep the ship from sinking beneath them.

Fortunately they sighted another schooner; a lumber laden ship from Miramichi bound for Liverpool, England. The ship-wrecked crew were taken off the wallowing *Agnes* and it was abandoned at sea. McGrath found a passage to Waterford, Ireland, and there he located a ship sailing to Newfoundland.

In the spring of 1830, Thomas McGrath took command of the schooner *John*, headed north for the annual seal hunt. The ship cleared from King's Cove, although another source says it sailed out of Trinity, bound "for the ice."

It is known the *John* carried a crew of nineteen from Bonavista Bay, one of whom was Barnabas Moss from Open Hall, a town located a few miles from King's Cove. Moss left a large family of nine or ten children. One of children, Jacob Moss, married Elizabeth Prince of Princeton and resided in Princeton.

This tale of the schooner *John*, albeit incomplete, was reported in the newspaper *Fisherman's Advocate* of May 10, 1929, by Joseph Henry Moss of Eastport, the grandson of Barnabas Moss. Joseph Henry was the census taker in Eastport in 1911.

The people lived in hope that nineteen men missing from the vessel *John* would return; perhaps a passing ship had picked them up (as had happened with the *Agnes*) or they may have been stranded on some distant shore. But hopes were dashed when they heard old Mrs. Barrett of 'Longshore' tell how she saw the crew of the *John* walk down the harbour one night in silent single file and disappear into the sea below her house.

The tale of tragedy was repeated many years later when another King's Cove vessel disappeared. On December 6, 1876, the schooner *Edward* was ready to leave St. John's for King's Cove. It was deeply laden with winter supplies for Michael Murphy & Sons. Perhaps it was a quirk of fate or some unfathomable oddity, but if the anchor had not fouled on bottom when the crew prepared to set sail, the ship would have reached Catalina before the storm of early December 7 broke.

Dan Murphy, son of the owner, was in St. John's and, when he heard the schooner was delayed, went to the waterfront. He told the crew to slip the chain and to attach a buoy to it. Murphy would hire a diver in the morning to retrieve the anchor.

But the crew worked at retrieving the anchor and in an hour it was freed from the bottom. Just as it was being lifted, a fourteen-year-old student from Bishop Field College, Arch Skiffington of Tickle Cove, near King's Cove, hurried up to the schooner. He was anxious to get home for the holidays and asked for a passage. The crew was reluctant, but Dan Murphy, who had once been a college student himself at St. Bonaventure, knew what a refusal would mean to the boy.

He said to Skiffington, "Certainly, my boy," and said to the skipper, "Make him as comfortable as you can."

That was the last piece of news on the forty-five ton *Edward*. Relatives and loved ones could only speculate that the storm must have overtaken the schooner when it was halfway across Trinity Bay. The crew all had family ties: Captain Michael McGrath, his son James, an older and veteran seaman William Doyle (grandfather of Gerald S. Doyle of the Doyle Radio News Bulletin), James Flynn and his son Daniel. Daniel was not part of the crew, but had gone to St. John's on *Edward* to purchase a violin. Also lost was passenger and student Arch Skiffington, son of Adam Skiffington. James Flynn was the father of M.T. Flynn, a businessman-shipowner of Marystown and progenitor of the family name in that town.

The storm lasted over twenty-four hours causing folks at King's Cove to say, "The *Edward* is gone down. It could never stand this storm." Relatives waited and hoped, but the King's Cove schooner never appeared.

No doubt there were other vessels in later years that gave King's Cove people anxiety and despair, but these two unsolved mysteries of the sea exemplify the hardships of those who chose to go down to the sea in ships.

Six Brothers LeShane of Lower Island Cove

Date:	*05,1883*
Location:	*Trinity Bay*
Fatalities:	*13*
Remarks:	*Disappearance of "Six Brothers"*

On May 25, 1883, thirteen men sailed from Lower Island Cove for the east side of Trinity Bay, a two hour run each way. The wind was fair; they hoisted sail and left. They would load wood aboard their 26-ton schooner *Six Brothers* and return the same day.

Photo of headstone to victims of *Six Brothers* disaster. In a Lower Island Cove churchyard a tower headstone commemorates the thirteen victims of the *Six Brothers*. Photo courtesy William Pellerin, Exeter, New Hampshire

Since no foul weather was predicted and it was a fine, clear day for sailing, no problems were anticipated. As they were not expected to be gone long, perhaps few good-byes were said. No tears were shed at their leaving; that would come later with full realization that they would never be seen again by those left behind.

The *Six Brothers* never reported back into Lower Island Cove. No doubt others went to search, but no wreckage nor bodies were ever located. Six LeShane (or LeShana) brothers owned the vessel; two who were ill, stayed home but Frederick, Willis, Philemon and Noah were lost. They and the others were all residents of Lower Island Cove. William Wheeler left a wife and seven young children.

LOST ON *SIX BROTHERS*	
Frederick Leshana	age 36
Willis LeShana	age 32
Philemon Leshana	age 30
Noah Leshana	age 26
John Cummins	age 20
Eli Reed	age 24
Peter Snelgrove	age 20
Azariah Lewis	age 38
Eli Lewis	age 21
John G. Lewis	age 37
William Wheeler	age 36
Peter Diamond	age 20
Thomas Garland	age 20

One of his sons was John Wheeler, killed in the explosion on the S.S. *Viking* on March 15, 1931.

In Great Gloom

Date:	*11,1896*
Location:	*Gulf of St. Lawrence?*
Fatalities:	*10-15*
Remarks:	*The "Clio" and "Lady May" Disappear*

In November 1896 a short piece of shipping news indicating the loss of three Carbonear ships appeared in an island newspaper. It documents the community's anxiety for the ships which were long overdue.

Very few towns in Newfoundland and Labrador suffered more from losses at sea than Carbonear. Reports of marine disasters prior to1850s are obscure, but accounts, either lengthy or brief, of most losses the second half of the twentieth century have been recorded. From the year 1838 when John Rorke started his Labrador-based fish exporting business in Carbonear, to its closure in the 1970s, his ships and ship losses are more or less documented.

One of his first vessels to disappear with crew was the brigantine *Muriel* while crossing the Atlantic on a westward voyage to Carbonear (see page 26). John Rorke & Sons schooner *Rose* was lost with captain James Kennedy and thirty-seven passengers and crew while returning from the Labrador fishery on October 15, 1877. When one adds the subsequent losses of *Snowbird, Clio* and *Beatrice*, a staggering total of approximately sixty lives were taken by the sea on Rorke's ships alone. For the longer and strange tale of Rorke's *Snowbird*, see Chapter 5 of my *Between Sea and Sky*.

Hardship, grief and anxiety reached a peak in early 1896. On January 28 the brief, but poignant article **"Missing Vessels"** which pondered the fate of three Carbonear ships, appeared in *The Daily News*, saying:

MISSING VESSELS

Carbonear is in great gloom. The *Argonaut* belonging to Duff & Balmer was lost with all hands some weeks ago. The *Lady May* belonging to Simpson & Black left Prince Edward Island 27 days ago, bound for St. John's and nothing has been heard of her since. Now there is considerable anxiety about the *Clio*, Captain James, belonging to Hon. John Rorke, which is 56 days out from Gibraltar. Whilst there is no hope for the *Argonaut*, and little for the *Lady May*, there is no reason for undue anxiety for the *Clio*.

*A*rgonaut loaded codfish at Labrador in late November 1895 and sailed for Halifax, but was never heard from again. The six crew were from Carbonear, four of whom are known: Captain William Luther, his brother and mate George Luther, John Burke and William Long.

There are some family memories passed on about the latter crewman, William Long. He left a wife, Elizabeth (Pike) Long, and 3 children. A fourth child, Whilomena, was born seven months after the ship was given up. It was said by the Long family that the *Argonaut* was leaky, but the previous owner didn't tell the new owners, the Duffs, about the hard-to-find leak. It was also believed the ship left Nova Scotia with coal and probably foundered on the voyage home.

As it turned out the anxiety for Rorke's *Clio*, a vessel only one year old, was well- founded. Sailing with a cargo of salt dry fish on consignment for Spain, it reached Gibraltar safely and loaded salt at Alicante, Spain, in late November. In January 1896 there was, as the *The Daily News* pointed out, no reason for anxiety for the lives of *Clio*'s young Carbonear sailors. It was a false hope - Captain Mark James, mate Thomas Joy, cook Alfred Locke, bosun G. W. Pike, sailors Richard Ellis, Samuel Pike and Bernard Murphy, were lost with their ship.

*S*impson & Black's 59-ton *Lady May* was built in 1878 at Little Bras d'Or, Nova Scotia, by Simon Deveau. Five years later it ran into trouble on the high seas as noted by the North Sydney *Herald*, June 14, 1883. *Lady May* sailed from Little Bras d'Or early June for St. John's with a cargo of oats owned by J.H. Christie and Sons. Two weeks later it had not reported, but the schooner must have had a difficult passage in high winds as it eventually arrived safely.

In 1886 John Steer's firm at St. John's bought *Lady May* for $1250.00. The schooner was getting old and in the financial difficulties brought on by the advent of the bank crash in Newfoundland, *Lady May* was sold to Simpson and Black of Carbonear. That fall it was sent to Prince Edward Island for a load of vegetables and other shop supplies.

At that time Captain Samuel Burke, like many other skippers and seamen, was unemployed and Mr. Black asked Burke to find a crew to make the trip. He did, asking his brother James to go as mate, along with seamen William Moores and two other men. All five crew were married and had relatively large families.

It was almost Christmas 1895 before the schooner left Newfoundland, but it reached Prince Edward Island and loaded its cargo. It was last sighted and spoken to as it passed though Canso Strait early January. Captain Burke, seeing the unsettled weather, anchored off Canso for awhile then left for home. Authorities and loved ones in Carbonear grew anxious and, upon enquiry over its lateness, it was learned it left Canso January 2. Nothing was heard of the vessel again and the rest is pure speculation.

Rorke's foreign-going vessel *Clio*. In 1896 it disappeared, taking seven Carbonear men with it. Photo courtesy Maritime History Archive, MUN, St. John's

It is known a tremendous storm swept southern Newfoundland on January 5 and 6. About that time *Lady May* would have been off St. Mary's Bay. There are those who think Burke and his crew were lost on Christmas Day; others say January 5 at the dreaded St. Mary's Keys (often called The False Keys by sailors).

The Burkes left two widows and seven children. William Moores, of Freshwater, a town near Carbonear, was married to Laura (Butt) Moores and had seven children: Thomas Heal Moores, Elizabeth, Stephen, Haywood, Ada, William, Albert, Eugene and Ernest. It is believed that while the breadwinner William was away at sea, several of Laura's infant children were stricken with diphtheria and died. Today the story of *Lady May* is kept alive by William Moores' descendants Judy (Moores) Patey and Audrey Moores.

The Ship That Never Returned

Date:　　　*03,1892*
Location:　　*Gulf of St. Lawrence?*
Fatalities:　*7*
Remarks:　　*The "Grover Cleveland" Still Unreported*

Ships are overdue, perhaps lost at sea. Worried relatives wait and hope. After a certain period and no word of missing ships is forthcoming, worry turns to grief. Many people never give up hope and rely on the adage, "There is hope from the sea, but none from the grave."

With human remains and burial, there is closure and finality; alas, with the vast ocean, there is always a thought of salvation. Families cling to the idea a crew may have escaped in the lifeboat or dory, or the vessel became dismasted and was still driving about the ocean. Perhaps the unlucky mariners will be rescued by a passing vessel and will end up in some foreign land safe and sound.

Often an "anxiety" report - a brief notice that a ship is missing appears-in the paper. It may not give many details for, who knows, perhaps the vessel will turn up after all. Eighty days after a St. Mary's Bay schooner sailed and still had not reported, an "anxiety" report appeared in the local papers. It read simply: **The Worst is Feared.**

By April 20, 1892, loved ones, ship owners and friends were concerned about the banking schooner *Grover Cleveland*. It sailed from Mount Carmel, St. Mary's Bay, around March 1 or 2, carrying a load of fish for Boston. If it arrived in Boston, someone would certainly have telegraphed or written home. But nothing had been heard from the vessel and most people feared it ran head on into a fierce gale which swept Newfoundland's west coast on March 4. That would have been about right - it was about one or two day's sail from St. Mary's Bay.

That terse first indication of fear mentioned only the Captain's name - James Day - and that *Grover Cleveland* carried six Newfoundland men. A month later or over seventy days after

Grover Cleveland sailed away, words appearing in public print bore an ominous finality:

Ships That Never Return

There have been many ships which sailed out from island ports and have never returned; their fate is still unknown. Considering the vast amount of sea commerce which arrived and departed Newfoundland and Labrador in the era between the 1850s to 1950, perhaps the number of missing ships is small in the aggregate. Another supposed disappearance for 1892 was Bowring Brothers' barquentine *Ulster*, under Captain Sheckel, which had left St. John's for Liverpool.

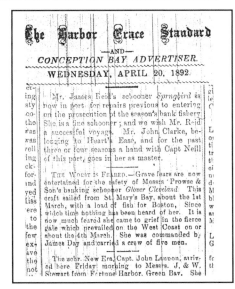

Now, lost in the misty past, it is not clear where the schooner *Grover Cleveland* was built and christened, or its dimensions. It certainly carries the name of the 22nd (and 24th) president of the United States, but how and why it came under the registry of R. Prowse and Sons is not known. Robert Prowse had a mercantile business in St. John's.

Although *Grover Cleveland*'s crew signed on at Prowse's city premises, most were from St. Mary's Bay and area: Captain Day, bosun William Singleton, cook Thomas Power, seamen William Ryan and John Bishop, all of Salmonier, (today's Mount Carmel) in St. Mary's Bay. Seaman

Daniel Ryan belonged to Holyrood, a town later renamed St. Vincent's - and seaman Thomas Ryan resided in St. John's.

It is not clear if the ship *Ulster* ever reported, but descendants of *Grover Cleveland*'s know the latter is a ship that never returned. No human tongue can tell the lonely and desperate days and the vigilant nights, praying, wishing, hoping.

No Village Bell Shall Toll for Them

Date:	*?,1903*
Location:	*Between Old Shop and St. John's*
Fatalities:	*6*
Remarks:	*Old Shop Schooner Unreported*

It is thought that the name Old Shop, a community located along a bank on the west side of Dildo Arm, Trinity Bay may have gotten its name from "old chop." For many years the area was used by winter people of Trinity to cut ships' timbers. In his diary Trinity merchant Benjamin Lester referred to dispatching winter crews to Old Shop. Old Shop was also a fishing community and, as often happened to seafaring communities, a sea disaster once touched this town.

In the fall of 1900, Joshua Reid, a boat builder who had moved to Dildo Arm, Trinity Bay, from Sound Island, Placentia Bay, began to build a schooner at Spread Eagle, a small town about two miles from Old Shop and since abandoned. The building materials that he used were from the tall tree stands near Old Shop and, in the spring, the schooner was launched and given the name *Speedwell*.

For five years the *Speedwell* engaged in a successful fishery at Cape St. Mary's and helped give prosperity to Old Shop. In the fall of 1902, disaster struck the *Speedwell* as it was making its way to St. John's with a load of fish. A storm came up as the schooner

The poem from *Morning Courier* "The Sailor's Grave"

was crossing Conception Bay and it was never seen again. The men lost on the schooner were Simon Pretty of Dildo, Joshua Reid and his son Edmund, John Reid, Tom Mercer, and William Smith all from Old Shop. The loss of the life and supplies caused untold hardship for the community that winter.

Elizabeth "Lizzie"(George) Reid, Joshua's wife, always believed the crew was shipwrecked on an island and would return someday. She expected them back. She was left with six children. There were precious few ways to make a living in outport Newfoundland in those days, so the Reid family, chiefly the step-father, built another ship, the *Elsie R*(Reid) in later years, and continued to follow the whims of the sea.

Ariel image of Old Shop Spread Eagle. Old Shop, right, and Spread Eagle, centre.

Perhaps there is no one in Newfoundland and Labrador who has collected the names of all the missing ships that have sailed from this province's ports. Certainly there must be scores and scores that sailed out and never returned, many of which may never be documented. And when one thinks of how many men, women and children were lost with them, the words of Rudyard Kipling in the poem "We have Fed Our Sea" ring true:

If blood be the price of Admiralty,
Lord God, we ha' paid in full.

One of the Worst Clamities at Ferryland Head

Date: 12,1903
Location: Ferryland Head
Fatalities: 6
Remarks: Danish Ship Wrecked at Ferryland

The Ferryland Head lighthouse keeper, William Costello, came into Ferryland on his horse and cart to inform the town of the grim details of a tragic wreck near Ferryland Head. The head, located at the end of a narrow peninsula at the south side of Ferryland harbour, is connected to the mainland by a narrow isthmus. The lighthouse is about a mile from Ferryland. Costello covered the distance quickly in case any shipwreck survivors were on the rocks, but he was not optimistic. He reported:

> Vessel wrecked. Lost with all on board, I figure.
> Out near the head on Burnt Head Point. One of the
> worst ever and God knows, there's been many over
> the years. If there are any survivors on this one,
> it'll be a miracle. (*The Daily News* December 11,
> 1903)

Costello had first seen this wreck on Saturday morning, December 5, 1903, just as dawn was breaking. From his view at the lighthouse, he couldn't tell what schooner it was nor how many crew were aboard. When Costello broke the news in Ferryland, several people quickly went into action and prepared to go to the cliffs for a rescue or to recover bodies.

Since the early 1870s when its beams first flashed out a warning beacon, the Ferryland Head lighthouse had weathered many a storm. Its light, 200 feet above sea level, has a range of 14 miles. Head light keepers at Ferryland in the early years included Michael Kearney, Patrick Keough and four generations of Costellos who tended the light from 1875-1970.

There had been other shipwrecks over the years. About twenty years previous another dramatic rescue occurred at Ferryland Head when on August 6, 1883, Assistant Lightkeeper Philip Keough of Ferryland, singlehandedly saved Captain Disney

Photo of Ferryland Head 1909

and the crew of the barquentine *Octavia*. It was bound from St. John's to Sydney. For his bravery Keough was awarded a silver medal by Sir Frederick B.T. Carter on behalf of the Royal Humane Society.

Now in late 1903, another disaster. William Costello relayed the news of shipwreck to the local magistrate and to Ferryland's Assistant Collector of Customs, W.T.S. Carter. Four men - John Keefe, Valentine Keefe, Robert Shannahan and James Barnable -

Ferryland Head light and dwelling house in 1909. A road from Ferryland Beach to the light was constructed by St. John's stone mason contractors Campbell and Burridge. Originally the 46-foot high tower was made of brick. The lantern and light apparatus were supplied by Messrs. D.& T. Stevenson of Edinburgh. It was fueled by a system of kerosene lamps. In 1892 the tower was entirely sheathed in iron. An electric light replaced the kerosene lamps in 1931. Photo and information courtesy Canadian Coast Guard "Lighthouses of Newfoundland and Labrador"

quietly mustered around, readied their ropes and gear and set out for the lighthouse.

Soon they saw quantities of wreckage, consisting of spars, sails, deck gear and clothing, presumably belonging the crew. There was no lifeboat and no sign of the crew to be seen all up and down the coast and, at first, the Ferryland men concluded they had rowed into some harbour.

John Keefe then ventured down over the cliff as far as possible to see what other belongings of the wreck might be drifting about. He saw the body of a man, nearly naked, wedged in a gulch about 150 feet from where he stood.

He called to the other three, "Boys, there's the body of a dead man below here. We must try and get him." They soon were

Bankers Arrive. 7

Ferryland harbour was a high traffic area for banking schooners. This *Evening Telegram* list for July 8, 1915, shows which schooners put into Ferryland for bait or repairs.

Since Monday last the following vessels put into Ferryland from the Grand Banks, some of them damaged and others for a supply of bait:—

Name.	Catch.
Castle Carey	250 qtls.
Kasara	200 "
Marjorie Inkpen	170 "
Grace Day	150 "
Veta Covrad	400 "
Linus A...	200 "
Oronate	300 "
Deverning	150 "
Stella	100 "
Effie M. Prior	200 "
Arine	200 "
Aronus P. Smith	260 "
Effie M. Petite	200 "
Lillian O.	200 "
Allan A. Rose	150 "
Flora Nickerson	200 "
Vilot Courtney	100 "
Lindo Tibbo	100 "
Arginia	500 "
Helen B. Morne	150 "
Valonia	200 "
B. P. Doningoes	150 "
Chesley Raymond	200 "
Lucia	100 "

ready to help. Keefe put a rope around his waist and the others helped lower him down the side of the cliff. After five attempts battling with the sea as it rushed in and out the gully, Keefe reached the body and secured it from the hungry sea. He tied a rope around the arms and the body was slowly pulled up over the cliff face.

By this time others had gathered at the cliff top including John W. Costello, Thomas Sullivan, James Keough and Daniel Keefe, who all helped recover that body; then another which was found later in the morning. Before the Saturday passed a total of five were found, one of whom was a colored man. Another body was almost completely severed in two pieces and one wore a ring with the initials J.E. Eventually the remains were respectfully interred at Ferryland.

The wreckage at first puzzled the Ferryland men. It did not appear to belong to a Newfoundland nor an English vessel. On three boards were indistinct words, torrens, touekehyt and besti. These were subsequently identified as the Danish words for certain rooms on a ship - cabin, chartroom, forecastle and so on.

By Monday, December 7, Customs Officer Carter was able to tell the Minister of Marine and Fisheries in St. John's the vessel was the *Sigrid* and that some of its official papers had been found near the wreck. It was from Denmark, registered at 80 ton and carried five crew.

Soon details of *Sigrid*'s final voyages became clear. The fore and aft rigged ship and its captain, N. Petersen, were well-known in Newfoundland waters. A. S. Rendell and Company

The Eveni
AWFUL DISASTER
Loss of the "Sigrid."
Danish Schooner Runs Against Bluff Cliff and All on Board Lose Their Lives.

of St. John's acted as its local agent. In late 1902 *Sigrid* came to St. John's to load fish for Oporto. In June 1903, it brought sugar for A.H. Murray's business and on July 24, left St. John's to go to Philip Templeman's premises at Bonavista to get a cargo of fish destined for Europe.

On November 7, 1903, *Sigrid* sailed in ballast from Spain, but it could only be surmised that as the ship approached Newfoundland's southern shore in early December, there was dense fog. It sailed straight into a cliff face at Ferryland Head and in a few minutes went to pieces in the heavy sea. Waves pounding and recoiling from the cliff would have made it impossible to launch a lifeboat. Most of the bodies among the rocks were terribly mutilated.

The process of identification was made easier for in St. John's at the time were other Danish ships. Three captains - Lindergard of the *Carl*, Yensin of the *Nemesis* and Rasmussen of the schooner *Rasmussen* - went to Ferryland to identify bodies and to collect personal effects of the victims which would be sent to Denmark.

The final words on one of Ferryland's worst calamities came from a local newspaper:

Kind-heartedness and pluck are characteristics always associated with our fishermen. While it is not unusual for the people of Ferryland to put forth humane effort, the chronicling of that performed by those who recovered the bodies of the unfortunate seamen drowned from the Danish ship *Sigrid* is not less notable...

Nothing definite on how the ship was lost, but loved ones have been recovered and with decency and reverence laid to rest in God's Acre in Ferryland.

This monument to the captain and sailors of the *Sidrid* was erected in Ferryland after the wreck. In time it became obscured by brush and earth. In the mid-1990s descendants of Captain N. Petersen arranged to have the monument restored. Through the efforts of the Ferryland Historical Society and Charles and Maxine Dunne, it now stands proudly overlooking the sea and Ferryland Head.

As a further note of marine interest, on February 13, 1904, about three months after the loss of *Sigrid*, lightkeeper William Costello, aged 65, lost his life near Ferryland Head when he fell from a cliff and was killed. He was survived by his wife, three sons and a daughter.

Somewhere between Seldom and Change Island

Date: *11,1920*
Location: *Seldom-Change Island*
Fatalities: *6*
Remarks: *"General Horne" Fails to Make a Short Run*

In *The Book of Newfoundland, Volume IV*, page 84, there is a brief statement (in an article written by Andrew Horwood) of a curious disappearance of a Newfoundland ship. It says, "When the chance offered the *General Horne* left for the short trip between Seldom and Change Island; a trip often made in a trap skiff." The vessel never completed this short journey; its crew disappeared from the ken of mankind.

In the fall of 1920, the tern schooner *General Horne* completed the approximate 2500 mile ocean voyage from Europe to Newfoundland. It was a smooth voyage from Cadiz, Spain, and deeply laden with fishery salt, the schooner put into Catalina. From there it sailed to Seldom-Come-By to await a favorable wind to push it through the Stag Harbour Run and to Change Island. It did reach Seldom, according to the people there, and then departed for Samuel Harris's branch business at Change Island, Newfoundland, where it could have discharged the salt.

Vessel Missing.

The Deputy Minister of Custo has received the following mess from the Sub-Collector at Gr: Bank: "Schooner General Hor owned by S. Harris, Ltd., left Catal on Nov. 20th for Change Islands has not since been reported. Fe for the safety of the vessel are tertained as per report to me fr her owners."

As Horwood states, it wasn't far - about 20 kilometres - and one made by hundreds of times by fishermen in small boats like a trap skiff. The *Horne*, at 107 foot long, was completely seaworthy and had made many voyages from Europe to Newfoundland and back. It was owned in Grand Bank on Newfoundland's south coast and had journeyed from there to Notre Dame Bay often to load or discharge fish or salt.

Weeks passed and concerned relatives anxiously awaited news and reports from the tern schooner, but the *Horne* never sailed into any port. Captain Berkley Rogers, Grand Bank; William Brooks, Randall Mayo, both of Fortune; Otto Ledrew, Change Island, and two other seamen were aboard.

On December 17, 1920, this anxiety (short notice saying a vessel is overdue) report appeared in *The Evening Telegram*:

The Deputy Minister of Customs has received the following message from the Sub-Collector at Grand Bank: "Schooner General Horne, owned by S. Harris, Ltd, left Catalina on November 20th for Change Island and has not since been reported. Fears for the safety of the vessel are entertained as per report to me from owners."

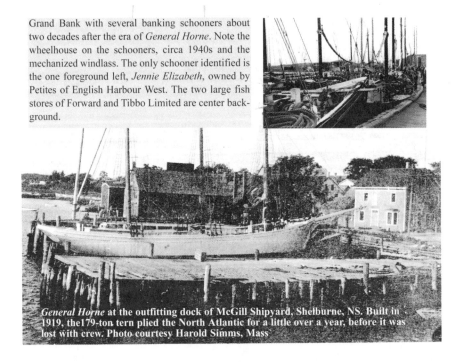

Grand Bank with several banking schooners about two decades after the era of *General Horne*. Note the wheelhouse on the schooners, circa 1940s and the mechanized windlass. The only schooner identified is the one foreground left, *Jennie Elizabeth*, owned by Petites of English Harbour West. The two large fish stores of Forward and Tibbo Limited are center background.

General Horne at the outfitting dock of McGill Shipyard, Shelburne, NS. Built in 1919, the 179-ton tern plied the North Atlantic for a little over a year, before it was lost with crew. Photo courtesy Harold Simms, Mass

There were at least two sightings of a derelict believed to be *General Horne*. While steaming westward at latitude 49.01 north, longitude 17.35 west, in March1921, the British steamship *Housatonic* came upon the grim ruins of an unknown derelict off the British Isles. It consisted of the remains of the poop and part of the main deck of a dismasted, waterlogged sailing vessel. Part of a name **RAL HORNE** and the port of registry, **St. John's**, could barely be seen on the stern which was partially submerged.

Housatonic reported that the vessel's cargo appeared to be timber, and the derelict was about 150 feet long. However, the wreck was so unseaworthy that to tow it to port for further examination was impossible.

Confirmation that the *Horne* was lost with crew was reported not only by the British liner but also by the banking schooner, *Marion Belle Wolfe* captained by John Thornhill of Grand Bank, the home port of the missing tern schooner.

Marion Belle Wolfe, which had several crewmen from *General Horne*'s home port of Grand Bank, was fishing near the Virgin Rocks in early March. Someone sighted a drifting hulk. Although there was a dangerous swell, a dory from *Marion Belle Wolfe* approached the overturned derelict. By then the cargo of salt had melted and the debris floated high. Barely visible below water line, the men from schooner could distinguish its name; no remains of her crew were ever seen.

Except for the captain's name, no crew list for *General Horne* was ever presented in local papers, and it is only by word of mouth that some of the other sailors are known. Otto LeDrew was married to Emma Belle Pomeroy. It is noted in the Methodist parish records of Herring Neck, Otto was "Drowned at Sea" on November 20, 1920. His memorial church service was performed by Rev. Wilfred James Woolfrey. Captain Rogers was married and left a wife and three children, the youngest, two years old.

The *Pendragon* Trail

Date:	*07,1914*
Location:	*Off the Tip of the Great Northern Peninsula*
Fatalities:	*8*
Remarks:	*Northern Arm Schooner Disappears*

The Pendragon Trail, a popular hiking route near Northern Arm, Notre Dame Bay, has the roots of its name in the tale of the schooner *Pendragon*, owned in Northern Arm in 1914. There were scores of schooners owned in that area over the years, but the name *Pendragon* remains with us, for its demise is one shrouded in mystery and tragedy.

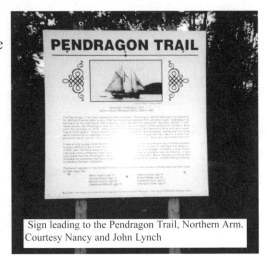

Sign leading to the Pendragon Trail, Northern Arm. Courtesy Nancy and John Lynch

In 1914 the dangers of navigation in the Labrador fish trade - rocks, shoals, ice, adverse weather - struck home to the Newfoundland fishing fleet. The schooner *Pendragon*, owned by Henry Evans of Northern Arm, Notre Dame Bay, had not reported into any port normally frequented by schooners bound north - St. Julien's, Conche, St. Anthony. Nor had it arrived on the southern Labrador coast or at its ultimate destination, Saglek Bay.

Pendragon built 32 years previosly was an old schooner. Built in Essex, Massachusetts, in 1882 it was 77 feet long, 22 feet wide. By 1908 its registry changed to John J. O'Neill of Burin, Newfoundland, and then to Doctor Wilfred Grenfell, the missionary doctor of Labrador. Grenfell sold the 75-ton schooner to Captain Henry Evans.

Captain Evans, according to the book *For the Love of a Woman* by Calvin Evans, was late getting under way for the

Crew of Northern Arm Schooner
***Pendragon*, Lost July 1914**

Capt. Henry Evans	age 57
George Malcolm Evans	age 11
Benson Evans	age 23
Gladstone Manuel	age 19
Jethro Evans	age 24
Frederick Ginn	age 31
Georgina Cook	age 21
Robert Blake	age 36

Labrador in 1914. It was past mid-July when he sailed out of Northern Arm. He had seven others with him, including his eleven-year-old son, George Malcolm Evans, and a lady cook for the fishing crew. *Pendragon* carried a good load with a full set of fishing gear, oil drums, many hogsheads of salt, two trap skiffs on deck and towed a 25 to 30 foot fishing boat behind.

The weather near the tip of the Great Northern Peninsula turned nasty and a schooner from Twillingate behind *Pendragon* put into a safe harbor. Somewhere near the Quirpon Run, north of St. Anthony, *Pendragon* disappeared.

Near the end of July someone found wreckage near Great Brehat, a fishing settlement on the northeast shore of the Great Northern. Mr. Noah Simms of St. Anthony relayed the information to the St. John's papers and on July 31, 1914, a snippet of information appeared in *The Daily News*:

Wreckage Found! Is There a Loss?
Yesterday forenoon (July 30) the Marine and Fisheries Department received the following message from Mr. Simms of St. Anthony: "A large motor trap boat and schooner's gaff topsail picked up at Great Brehat; it is probable a schooner has been lost."

Instructions were at once forwarded to make all inquiries possible as to the supposed wreck but up to last night no further information had been received.

The first indication of disaster was *Twillingate Sun* rumor that the Pendragon was missing; a few days later, on October 17, most people realized the schooner was lost with crew.

The account did not speculate to which schooner the debris belonged. However, *Pendragon* did not return to Northern

117

Arm in the fall. No one had tidings of it on the Labrador coast and, since it was known Evans' schooner had carried trap boats on deck, relatives of the lost crewmen determined the wreckage must belong to *Pendragon*. Later an oil drum drifted ashore which was believed to be from the schooner.

World War One was officially declared in August, 1914, but it is unlikely *Pendragon* was sunk by enemy craft. Possibly it struck hidden reefs, shoals, possibly the Brehat Shoals, or swamped or capsized in a wind storm.

The Night Before Christmas

Date:	*12,1880*
Location:	*Off Port au Port*
Fatalities:	*5-6?*
Remarks:	*Search for the "Arabella" Crew*

Just before Christmas 1880, St. John's officials in charge of shipping received a telegram from the Bay of Islands on Newfoundland's west coast. It was signed by Captain George Shepherd, commander of a search party which had been sent to the west coast some days previously.

Shepherd and his ship had been chartered to investigate disturbing news that wreckage from several ships had been found in the wake of a great storm that swept the coastline from St. George's Bay to Cape Ray. Some of the debris indicated the ships were of large capacity. Thousands of deals (blocks of squared timber) were floating, and five bodies had been seen in the surf. On another part of the coast a large quantity of wheat in bags was found in a landwash. (One ship wrecked in this storm was the New Brunswick vessel *Nonantum*, see Chapter Seven of *Salt Water Tales* in Volume Two).

In particular Captain Shepherd was to search for the crew of the St. John's schooner *Arabella*. It sailed from Chateau Bay, Labrador, with a full crew and one passenger, for the Bay of Islands, but had been caught in the gale. *Arabella* was located floating on its beam ends, i.e. lying flat on the water with masts parallel or near parallel to the water. Examination of the wreckage showed that the wind that upset the vessel must have been sudden for no attempt had been made to cut away the spars to get the ship back on an even keel.

One body was found on the derelict and that was later identified as one Thomas Parsons. The schooner's boat was gone and rumors around the Port au Port Peninsula suggested the remainder of the crew and one passenger attempted to reach shore. They never made it.

Some livyers on the shore saw a small boat with a number of people aboard heading toward Port au Port, a small village located on the isthmus between the peninsula and the mainland. In the gathering storm the boat disappeared from view and no one knew what had happened.

Captain Shepherd spent seven days in the general area, making a diligent search of the coastline and examining every creek and receding cove where a small boat could have made a landing. But nothing was seen.

In his final message back to St. John's Shepherd stated it would have been utterly impossible for any open boat to live while passing over the shoals and reefs that lay between the capsized schooner and the harbor of Port au Port.

Another Newfoundland ship caught in the storm was the barque *Fearless* en route from Labrador to New York. It had been "spoken to" or reported by another vessel 16 miles off Chatham, Massachusetts, leaking badly and with one set of sails ripped away completely and another set torn and shredded. The crew had been living on salt herring for eight days until the schooner *J.D. Adams* had furnished them with provisions.

Chapter 6
Strange and Unique

Although the names of people who helped me with leads to a
story can be found in the **Sources** section of *Salt Water Tales*, this
is a good place to acknowledge them personally. Many correspon-
dents sent letters, e-mails, phoned or we talked at various book
shows or venues and I thank each and every one.

Sometimes the information led to strange and unusual
tales and also to the sad and tragic. Peter Dicks of Corner Brook
told me how he had a "trip off" when his father and two brothers
sailed away for the last time on the schooner *Maria Margarita*.
There was not much in the local papers, but Peter's details were
fascinating. To supplement the *Maria Margarita* story, I also
thank Michael Caines who sent well-researched material on the
other ship and its uncanny encounter in this unique tale of the sea
- the fifth story in this chapter.

Where possible I cross-referenced personal information
with newspaper accounts and vice versa. The interviews and anec-
dotes not only provided interesting and valuable information on
ships, wrecks and the toll of human lives, but often gave valuable
insights into the folkways, customs, working and living conditions
of the times. Much of this information was also incorporated into
the tales of shipwrecks.

For example, my uncle, the late William Baker, explained
what it meant to be the junior or least experienced seaman on a
Newfoundland three-masted sailing ship. Once you had gone aloft
to tend the topsails and then had learned your duties and work,
you were assigned the foremast. The foremast, he said, was the
toughest, the most difficult mast to work. It was at the forefront of
headwinds and had the most rigging; therefore the greater amount
of work. I asked him why would they send a younger man or boy
up to the hardest sail to work? Because the older, senior men had
earned the right to take the mast with less work - the main or
mizzen. But he said when aloft in high winds, you had to hold on
with one arm and work with the other. And the sailors had a saying for this life-preserving principle: One arm for the company,
one arm for yourself.

He also told me of the strange superstitions: no black suit-
cases allowed aboard ship, no talk of pigs, never leave a hatch
cover upside down, no ship that he ever knew of (in Newfoundland at least) had ever been called after a fish and never whistle
aboard a vessel. The last piece of lore he reinforced with the old

saw, "Whistle to your plow, sing to your ship." And then he had
the ditty: The saucy hogs and Burin dogs,
                              Two turns on a stranger.
Of which, he said, there was no tune, no further verses, no mean-
ing, but it was bad luck to say it on a schooner.

Another gentleman, since passed away, recalled only one
verse of a song composed on the disappearance of the schooner
Jennie Duff of Grand Bank, missing with crew since 1917. Seems
as if one man had a premonition, based on his ideas of what con-
stituted a seaworthy vessel. He jumped ship at Fortune before it
sailed and walked the four miles home to Grand Bank. The song
says:

> Then Uncle Billy Fowler jumped out of his bunk,
> Saying, 'This very night I will pack up my trunk.'

Almost Insane

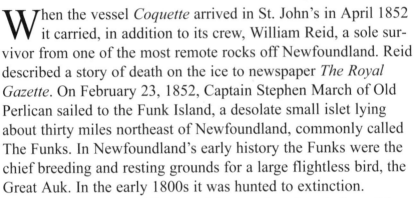

Date: 03, 1852
Location: The Funk Islands
Fatalities: 4
Remarks: Ghostly Sounds
on a Remote Island

When the vessel *Coquette* arrived in St. John's in April 1852 it carried, in addition to its crew, William Reid, a sole survivor from one of the most remote rocks off Newfoundland. Reid described a story of death on the ice to newspaper *The Royal Gazette*. On February 23, 1852, Captain Stephen March of Old Perlican sailed to the Funk Island, a desolate small islet lying about thirty miles northeast of Newfoundland, commonly called The Funks. In Newfoundland's early history the Funks were the chief breeding and resting grounds for a large flightless bird, the Great Auk. In the early 1800s it was hunted to extinction.

The newspaper *Evening Mercury*, in a description of the Funks in its October 8, 1888, issue, says that it is only possible to get on the Funks during a calm or a mild southerly wind and by landing on the northern side at a spot called "the bench." Even in the calmest weather a small boat at the bench will heave with the ocean swell 4 to 6 feet. At the bench is a narrow natural path about four feet wide that leads up for twenty feet. Of evidence of human occupation, the *Evening Mercury* says:

Evening Mercury.

ST. JOHN'S, OCTOBER 8, 1888.

FUNK ISLAND.

The Headquarters of the Great Auk.

Our readers will remember the accounts we published last year of the visit of the United States schooner *Grampus*, Captain J. W. Collins, on the service of the Fishery Commission. The expedition had for its object the search for the remains of the Great Auk on Funk Island. Most ....

Clipping of *Evening Mercury*
October 8, 1888

Crowning the summit of the island are the ruins of a stone hut. Years ago it was the winter quarters of a sealing party placed here to await the coming of the seals on the drifting ice of early spring. The experiment resulted fatally, for all save the cook were drowned while hunting. The cook, the sole survivor, was almost insane when rescued.

These were the five men landed on the Funks by Captain March in 1852 to hunt seals. If seals were plentiful the sealers would use the island as a base and enjoy a successful hunt spring after spring. Accordingly, for shelter, they built this rough stone hut.

One man, William Reid, stayed on the island to cook for the others: James Hopkins, his brother Jesse, William Croucher and Thomas Beckett - the latter probably belonged to Old Perlican.

The four sealers set off across the ice pans for the seals. Two hours after they were gone, Reid saw wind and waves were picking up and signaled for them to return. The sealers either didn't see the signal or were too busy to pay much attention to the cook's entreaty.

Eventually Beckett, seeing the deteriorating conditions, ran toward the Funks, but the pans had moved off leaving a narrow gulf of cold water between him and safety. Cook Reid threw a rope which Beckett caught, tied around his waist and the cook proceeded to pull him in. At the very moment when Beckett should have set foot on land, a wave burst on the two, washed the cook into a pool of water and Beckett was swept to sea never to be seen again.

Overhead photo of island. Plenty of white water surrounds the Funks. The Funks were considered to be an ever-present menace by mariners and seamen claimed several schooners that had vanished with all hands had run upon the small island. Today a colony of murres (or turrs) inhabit the cental ridge which may be the dark circle in the overhead view.

In the meantime the other three men stranded on the ice saw what had happened and went to the northwest part of the island thinking they could reach land from the "bench." But again high seas prevented them from reaching land. James Hopkins called to Reid asking him to launch the punt, but with the pounding combers that was impossible.

By this time the small pans were being ground into smaller and smaller pieces. Within a short time a wave struck the pan James and Jesse Hopkins and Croucher were on and they disappeared in the mad moll of ice and cold water. Reid was left alone on the Funk Island nearly a month until Captain J. Houlihan of the schooner *Coquette* came by on March 30 and rescued him. In terms of material possessions he had little: water, food, clothing, shelter. But the wind was a constant companion. It shrieked and howled over the jagged outcrops and toothed crags of granite day and night.

In later years Reid described the lonely hours, the whistling and moaning winds, wailing noises. In the long nights the sounds took on human intonations. The stranded man struggled with his conscience and wondered if he would stay sane until he was rescued.

An Extradorinary Tale of Survival and Co-incidence

Date:	10,1943
Location:	Strait of Canso
Fatalities:	3
Remarks:	A Newfoundland Seaman Survives a Shipwreck

Captain Joseph W. Emberley survived three shipwrecks; the last claimed all his crew except Emberley alone. A hard-working veteran seamen who had only one arm, Emberley was born in English Harbour East in Fortune Bay just before the turn of the twentieth century. He moved to Nova Scotia as a young man, became a captain, then a vessel owner and resided in Halifax.

Before recounting his extraordinary escape from the clutches of the sea and an accompanying tale of strange co-incidence, there's a story of fire aboard ship and Emberley's first shipwreck.

In mid-October 1931 and while five miles north northeast of the Sambro lightship off Halifax, a fire broke out on the auxiliary (powered by engine and/or sail) schooner *Catherine M* in command of Joseph "Joe" Emberley. It had sailed Sunday night for the banks and the next morning, as it was about to make its first set for fish near the lightship, the engineer discovered a fire below deck.

Apparently a small air compressor engine backfired, followed by a muffled explosion, and within moments the engine room was in flames. The crew put up a 20 minute fight, but the flames forced them off the schooner and out into their dories.

Crew of *Catherine M*, Burned October 21, 1931	
Sam Clarke	Halifax
Capt. Joseph W. Emberley	Dartmouth
engineer James Emberley, captain's brother	
Vincent Emberley, captain's son	
Clayton George	Queensport, NS
Angus McMasters	Dartmouth
Ignatius Oakey	Dartmouth

The Newfoundland Crew

James Bungay	Port aux Basques
cook Jack Butler	Placentia Bay
Hugh Fudge	Ramea
Robert Keeping Flat Island,	Placentia Bay
W. Kendell	Ramea
Henry Parsons	Burgeo
Charles Royle	Grand Bank
James Weymouth	Grand Bank

Engineer Vincent Emberley, the son of the captain, and Ignatius Oakey were the only crew in the after cabin; the others were in the forecastle preparing for work or having dinner. Because the fire was almost directly below the cabin, Vincent Emberley and Oakey both received burns - Emberley about the arms and Oakey's injuries were to his body and head.

The lightship crew saw the fire and sent word of *Catherine M*'s plight to C. H. Hosterman, agent for the Department of Marine. He contacted the Halifax Towboat Company which sent the tug *Samson*. The towboat poured a steady stream of water on the schooner from its fire hose and that, assisted by *Catherine M*'s crew, put out the flames. The Duncan's Cove lifeboat crew, commanded by Coxswain A.F. Holland, also went to the scene to help.

About noon the fire was under control and *Catherine M* was taken in tow for Halifax. Four feet of water sloshed about in the hold; the schooner was listing down by the head and it was completely gutted aft of the mainmast. Many in the crowd gathered at Mitchell and McNeil's wharf to view the schooner wondered how the vessel remained afloat in that condition.

By October 1943 and twelve years after the fire on *Catherine M*, Joe Emberley was the part owner and skipper of the sixty-ton schooner *Wally G*, built in 1910 at Grand Bank. On October 7 the schooner carried food and supplies from Halifax to the Magdalene Islands via the Strait of Canso. *Wally G* had three other crew: William Emberley, the captain's nephew, age 17; cook Albert Trenholm, 63, of Halifax and Alan MacDonald, 50, of Dartmouth. MacDonald had shares in *Wally G* and worked aboard as the managing owner.

About 5:30 a.m. the captain saw trouble ahead in the form of white breakers off White Point, Chedabucto Bay. In head winds and steaming along by engine power, the captain couldn't haul his vessel around fast enough and it piled onto the rocks. Within moments the schooner broke apart; MacDonald was swept over the side and never seen again. William Emberley was washed over the side by one of the waves, but managed to grab part of the stern section still afloat and held on for quite awhile. Captain Emberley had no idea what happened to Trenholm, who was at the wheel when *Wally G* struck. He was probably killed or drowned after impact.

The captain jumped to swim away from the tossing wreckage and found a large piece of deck planking. He held on after several minutes, then maneuvered over to where William still clung for his life. The boy was weakening fast in the cold October water. Because of its angle out over the water, there was no way he could climb up onto the wreckage and he was too cold and exhausted to swim for the captain's planks. Despite every entreaty of his uncle to hold on or swim to the planks, young William let go his grip and drowned before his uncle's eyes.

Although shocked and dismayed by his nephew's death

and by the sudden loss of two other shipmates, the captain soon regained his determination to stay alive. Despite having only one arm, Emberley had the courage and strength of a lion. After a struggle he managed to get the section of planking through the snarl of tossing wreckage and, in the easterly winds, his makeshift raft drifted slowly to sea.

When an occasional wave passed over the debris, which measured about six by six, Emberley increased his grip on the ring bolt attached to one of the planks. He knew he was still drifting in the much-frequented waterways off Canso and the Canso ship canal. By now morning had passed and the evening was windy and overcast. Often he would partly stand, holding on with his one arm, and scan the horizon for a passing ship. When he saw one, he took off his shirt and waved it.

Around five in the evening, after nearly twelve hours drifting, someone on the bridge of a steamer a mile or so away saw the wreckage and on a closer, longer look saw a man clinging to it, waving. The steamer stood by as a lifeboat went to rescue the exhausted castaway, Captain Joseph Emberley, of the schooner *Wally G*.

There is one other unusual twist to this tale of Captain Emberley. One of the men aboard the lifeboat was a childhood friend of Joe. Lee Hartigan had grown up in Rencontre East, located a few miles

Wally G at PEI
The cutwater schooner *Wally G,* tied on and awaiting produce at Montague, Prince Edward Island, showing the businesses Poole & Thompson, Ltd (left) and Johnstone's Flour and Feed (right). At this period in the career of *Wally G*, it was commanded by Newell Piercey of Fortune. Photo courtesy Janie Piercey, Fortune

from Emberley's hometown, and the two men knew each other, although they had not seen each other for many years. As soon as the survivor regained his warmth and his strength aboard the steamer, they were having a chat about common interests. Yet Emberley had other more traumatic thoughts: the loss of his ship-mates including his nephew, the wreck of his schooner and the sobering realization that he alone had survived for twelve hours on planks in Nova Scotia's cold October seas.

To Sleep; To Dream; To Survive

Date: *10, 1870*
Location: *Off Cape St. Gregory*
Fatalities: *2*
Remarks: *Survival Through*
                     a Remarkable Event

There's an old saying, "Search for one thing; find another." That's what happened in the spring of 2003 when this searcher scanned archival papers of September 1870 for news of the missing ship *H. Bradshaw* of Placentia. The search led on to December's papers; then a bold headline appeared, **"Perils of the Sea - Miraculous Escape"**.

"H.Bradshaw" stone. Little written evidence exists today of the loss of the schooner *H. Bradshaw* except this stone at Placentia which reads: Sacred to the Memory of Captain Frank Bradshaw Who was Lost at Sea Sept 7th , 1870, While in Command of the Schooner H. Bradshaw. Aged 38 Years. Also his companions F. Bradshaw, J. Fitzpatrick, James Foley, J. Murphy, Wm Kelley, T. J. Smith, H. Casmman.

It wasn't the account of the Placentia ship, but the story of the wreck of *William Inman*, a schooner from the Bay of Islands and the curious, yes miraculous, escape of several of its crew. When I read it I realized the tale was one of which I was familiar and had published several years ago. This longer and, perhaps, more accurate account is a re-rendering of my earlier story; this time with documented evidence from the newspaper of the day.

The story really begins in the late 1700s with a deserter from Britain's Royal Navy. William Gallop must have tired of the oppression when he deserted from a ship of the crown and risked hanging from a yardarm if caught. Undetected, he made his way to Lamaline, then Fortune at the tip of the Burin Peninsula.

William began a new life in Newfoundland, married Mary Kearley of Belleoram, Fortune Bay, and the couple raised eight children. In time, four of his children left Fortune, migrated to Newfoundland's West Coast, specifically the Codroy area, and married: Elizabeth (Gallop) Young, Jane (Gallop) Moore, Grace (Gallop) Martin and William Gallop, Jr.

But it was off Cape St. Gregory, about 200 kilometres north of Codroy, that the most unusual sea experience occurred to the descendants of William Gallop.

In October 1870, Captain John Gallop's vessel *William Inman* (incorrectly identified in an earlier story as *Eneman*, although it is easy to see how the multi-syllabic word could be reduced to Eneman) sailed from the Labrador to Halifax. It had a cargo of fish for James Butler and Company.

William Inman had six crew - Captain Gallop and his three brothers Henry, Joshua, Benjamin. Wilson Fiander was deck hand and a 15-year-old lad from England, Willie Owens, was cook.

The story of the wreck of *William Inman* and the singular tale of Captain Gallop came to Halifax through Captain Shaw of the schooner *Henrietta*. The story was so unique it was picked up and published in St. John's *Morning Chronicle* on December 13, 1870. Captain Shaw sailed to Halifax from the Bay of Islands and told the story of what had happened to *William Inman* to the newspaper.

Shaw said, "The latter ship had been shipwrecked and the crew escaped almost by a miracle."

While lying to off Cape St. Gregory *William Inman* was struck by a heavy sea. It fell over on its beam ends, the life boat was carried away as well as all other movable objects on deck.

129

Henry Gallop happened to be in the cabin when the ship listed out and drowned. The others tied themselves to the rigging to survive. In the long hours facing mountainous seas and harsh October winds, they expected any moment to be their last. They were several miles from shore and had no way of getting off the wreck.

According to the oral folk tales of the disaster, the English boy, Willie Owens who was injured when the ship capsized, died after the second day. His last words were pleas - should any of the others survive they must write his mother in England and tell her what happened. In the long wait for death hastened by low temperatures and rain the four survivors suffered from hunger and exposure.

For three days, the will to live kept them going a little longer. Each man slept a little, snatched a fitful nap, only to be awakened by cold wind, spray and hunger. According to the *Morning Chronicle*:

> Joshua Gallop, another brother of the captain, conceived the idea of making a canvas boat out of the foresail. His companions had little faith in the scheme, but as it seemed to be the only chance of escape, they went to work with a will, and soon completed one of the frailest boats in which life was ever entrusted to the ocean.

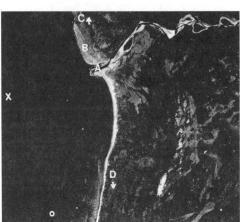

Map of Chimney Cove By 1870 only summer fishermen occupied Chimney Cove and the place was abandoned in the fall and winter. The first census shows a population of 100 - fisher families drawn by excellent lobster grounds off the coast. A is Chimney Cove (today an abandoned community); B is St. Gregory River; Trout River (C) is the nearest community some miles north; D, points to Bay of Islands; X where *William Inman* was lost.

From the tales the people tell of the miraculous escape, Joshua Gallop, in one of these moments of half sleep,

130

half consciousness while fighting to survive, got the idea of how to fashion a crude boat through a vivid and recurring dream.

The dream detailed how to make a boat from canvas from the sails. Joshua had no boat building experience, but so clear and real was his vision, he outlined it to the others. They were sceptical, reluctant and perhaps too close to death to care, but the dreamer finally convinced them to try. One man had a knife; thus in desperation the crew decided to fashion a small boat under Joshua's instructions.

Using canvas from the sails and wood from the bulwarks and railings lashed together with rope, they launched the frail craft. At first it sank under the weight of one man, but they replaced the heavy keel with a lighter one and amazingly, the makeshift cockleshell of a boat was deemed seaworthy. Using pieces of wood for oars, the survivors made the twenty miles from the wreck to Chimney Cove. Four days had elapsed since *Eneman* capsized.

Chimney Cove, located between Bay of Islands and Bonne Bay, was uninhabited, but a few shacks or rough homes lined the small cove. These were used by fishermen in the spring and summer. There was no food there, not a morsel, and it seemed at first the survivors had escaped death by exposure or drowning to die a longer torturous death through starvation. A tiny stream assuaged their thirst and in a garden the survivors dug a few turnips. Along the shoreline and in shallow water they found fish remains, or offal. Four days after landing and much strengthened, they set about improving their canvas boat for a long row to some inhabited town along the coast. Captain Shaw said (through the newspaper):

> On this not very palatable food they existed four days when a vessel hove in sight. They attracted the attention of the people on board, and a boat came ashore to them. The vessel proved to be *Burbeck*, Captain Hurst, bound to the Bay of Islands. The shipwrecked crew were taken on board and conveyed to that place.

The odd name for a Newfoundland vessel *William Inman* also came from a shipwreck. About two years previous, R.B. Currie, of West Dublin, Lunenburg, left that place in a small vessel owned by him. The little craft experienced bad weather, was driven off the coast and sustained great damage.

While it drifted about the ocean, unmanageable, an Inman steamer - the *City of Baltimore* - came in sight, saw the wreck, and ran down to it. Mr. Currie and all on board were rescued and taken to Liverpool, where Mr. William Inman showed them kind attention and sent them back to Halifax.

Mr. Currie marked his appreciation of his kindness by giving the name of *William Inman* to a vessel he was building - the same vessel now reported wrecked (and which had been bought by the Gallops at Halifax).

Through an amazing dream, a persistent Joshua Gallop, and a frail canvas boat the four survived a shipwreck. Their story is recorded in the *Book of Newfoundland*, Volume III - some of which is based on the oral retellings of the event - and also in a Newfoundland newspaper.

Freshwater Graves

Date:	*09,1927*
Location:	*Red Indian Lake*
Fatalities:	*None*
Remarks:	*Shipwreck on an Inland Lake*

Side paddle wheel steamer *Lady Mary* (above) at Red Indian Lake. Photo courtesy Bruce Neal

The demise and eventual disappearance of island ships! They met their ends in many a varied and odd way from piracy, fire, mutiny, disappearances, unexplained explosions, being rammed by ocean liners, chased and captured as rum runners by the American coast guard, collisions with icebergs, rocks, logs, dead whales, other ships. Some unfortunate schooners were struck by lightning or water spouts, shelled by enemy war vessels, crushed by Arctic ice or swallowed up by "August Gales" or the every hungry North Atlantic.

No one will ever know the exact number of ship losses, but the late Keith Matthews, who studied the subject for years at Memorial University, estimated that between ten thousand to fifteen thousand vessels have met their end in and around the waters of Newfoundland and Labrador.

However, the majority simply ran upon rocks or stranded on ledges, reefs or sunkers in nearly every cove, harbour, bay and headland around the coast. One of the oddest accidents to a local ship came compliments of a boulder or a tree stump which sank the *Fleetway*. It went to the bottom of Red Indian Lake while at anchor near Millertown, making *Fleetway* the only ship wrecked in a Newfoundland inland body of water.

Millertown, established by and named after businessman

Two Photos of *Fleetway*. The ship *Fleetway* (above) when it first arrived on Red Indian Lake, circa 1926. Below: The hulk of *Fleetway* much later in the winter ice of 1959. Both photos courtesy of Red Indian Lake Heritage Society Inc.

Lewis Miller who began sawmill operations there in 1900, is perhaps one of the earliest Newfoundland logging towns that is still a viable community. A few years later, when the Anglo-Newfoundland Development Company (AND) built a paper mill at Grand Falls, Millertown became headquarters for one of the company's four woods divisions. The great volume of logs needed for paper production were pushed or pulled on the lakes by powerful, lowset vessels. In the earliest days, side wheel paddle steamers did this heavy work and, according to local knowledge, when Miller constructed the sawmill in Millertown, he had the sidewheeler *Lady Mary* built there to move the logs.

Lady Mary was not elegant or swift; in fact it moved so clumsily and looked so strange the local people around Millertown called it "The Alligator." When the AND Company bought out Miller's operation they replaced the old and slow paddle steamer with another ship and *Lady Mary* was either beached or dismantled near the lake. A steam-driven propellor boat, the wooden *Fleetway*, took its place.

Fleetway, built on the shores of Red Indian Lake by the AND Company, was used to supply the logging camps around the lake and to move logs. For years Stanley Slade was in command of the vessel and he had his brother John with him as engineer. Fireman John Snook of Sunnyside, Trinity Bay, fuelled the steam engine with coal. Stanley Slade later became an train engineer with the railway.

Usually *Fleetway* was moored at Harbour Round on the shores of Red Indian Lake. Gordon Fogwill of Millertown had the job of keeping heat on all winter to prevent the ship from freezing up. *Fleetway* was well looked after, but an unusual event hastened its end.

In 1927 the AND Company built Exploits Dam on Red Indian Lake, raising the water level some 20 to 25 feet. Seeing there was more water in the lake than normal, the company anchored *Fleetway* in a sheltered cove on the north side of the lake near Millertown.

But that fall there was a less rain than usual or more water went over the falls. At any rate the water level went down slowly. *Fleetway* too dropped with the water until it came to rest on the bottom. "No harm done," so everyone thought. Those in charge and the caretakers were not too concerned until the rains came and *Fleetway* filled with water. It was time to pump the vessel out.

After three days of continuous pumping *Fleetway* was still full of water; there was no way of getting it out. At first Skipper Slade and the AND officials were puzzled. Several people tried to figure out what had happened to *Fleetway*. No one knew exactly, but the best guess was that when the ship settled on the bottom, a tree stump or a large boulder punctured the hull. The vessel could not be repaired nor refloated and was eventually abandoned.

To replace the wrecked vessel, the company purchased the steel tug *Fleetway II*, built in the Halifax and equipped with a powerful diesel engine. William Taylor of Millertown was put in command.

For years the shipwreck site of the old *Fleetway* became a favourite haunt of the young boys of Millertown who could easily reach the derelict on the winter ice. Today when the water level drops, the remains of its large steam engine can still be seen near the camp grounds on the side of the lake off the Buchans highway.

Fleetway was not the only vessel to find a freshwater grave in Newfoundland. Just after the 1900's, the paddlewheel steam tug *Dominion* laboured on Gander Lake. It was operated by the Phillips' lumber interests based in Maine. They established a mill at Barry's Brook near the mouth of the Gander River and Phillips' son, George Leamington Phillips (the namesake of the towns Point Leamington and Phillips Head), managed the Newfoundland end of the business.

Dominion herded logs until it eventually sank. Considering the great depth of Gander Lake, it is unlikely any remains of this ship will ever be found.

The Chilling Tale of Miss Glenburnie

Date:	*11?,1943*
Location:	*Newfoundland's West Coast*
Fatalities:	*4*
Remarks:	*Unexplained Events Aboard the Miss Glenburnie*

I magine, if you will, being at sea during a vicious storm, pondering which minute might be the last for the ship or yourself; only to have mysterious phantoms climb over the rail, looking for shelter from the storm.

The schooner *Miss Glenburnie* in 1940 as it nears completion in Silverton. Courtesy Everett Osmond via Ada Young

The uncanny tale of *Miss Glenburnie* begins some years before when Walter Young of Glenburnie, Bonne Bay, built the 70-ton banking and coasting schooner *Miss Glenburnie*. What better name for a vessel than to call it after the town of Glenburnie, located at the head of South Arm in Bonne Bay and named for its Scottish ancestry. Today Glenburnie-Birchy Head-Shoal Brook have combined to form a viable enclave within Gros Morne National Park.

Miss Glenburnie did well in the west coast fishery, crewed by Walter Young Sr., his three sons, John, Walter, Jr. and Heber Young. Another crewman was Walter's brother, John.

These men respected the sea and knew the Northwest coast can at times become dangerous and unforgiving, especially when winds came up. They well knew there is no safe harbour between Bonne Bay and Port Saunders to the north, a distance of approximately 100 miles.

By the early 1940s, many schooners like *Miss Glenburnie* were auxiliary vessels, that is they had a small engine usually with low horsepower, but could hoist sail when the wind was fair. Their speed at the best of times was under 10 knot. If a vessel was

in Port Saunders, the nearest sheltered port, Bonne Bay, was ten to twelve hours away.

Vessels usually waited in a port until the forecast predicted fair winds and good weather; thus Port Saunders became a harbour where crews of many vessels met and exchanged experiences.

Another schooner in this era which frequented Port Saunders was the coasting vessel *Maria Margarita* (incorrectly named *Marie Dicks* in local papers), owned by Joseph Dicks and named after this two daughters. And no doubt, since *Maria Margarita* also overnighted in Port Saunders, the Youngs of *Miss Glenb*urnie and the Dicks' men crossed paths and maybe had a conversation or two about trade, weather or family.

Typical jackboat of Placentia Bay, similar to *Maria Margarita,* is Tom Walters' *Alice & Edith Walters* of Paradise Sound - a vessel built in 1949. In Placentia Bay this type of small schooner was used in the inshore and on the Cape St. Mary's fishing grounds. The "jack", is often identified by its square stern and the rudder hung outside.

In 1957, the twelve-ton *Alice & Edith Walters* was used in lumber/land surveying and shows on deck Herman Denty, Eric Street and Capt. Tom Walters. Courtesy John Peacock, Navan, ON

The 30-ton *Maria Margarita* was built in Oderin around 1936 under the Commission of Government ship building bounty which paid builders 25 dollars a ton for their vessel. Master builder John Drake of Oderin designed the model and Captain Joe Dicks and his sons built his fishing schooner in the winter months.

By the late 1930s Skipper Dicks moved his family to Corner Brook on the west coast. His son Vincent already lived there. Skipper Dicks planned to fish on the west; he already had the gear aboard and a load of salt. When he saw the need for coasting vessels, he sold the gear and salt to Dunphy's business. With Dicks as master and his sons Joseph, Vincent and Peter crewing the coaster, the little vessel did well moving goods from Bonne Bay and Bay of Islands to Port Saunders.

In the fall of 1943 *Maria Margarita* made its final voyage. On the schooner that fall were Captain Dicks, his two sons Joseph and Vincent and John McLeod of Mount Moriah. The latter crewman replaced Peter Dicks, who had a trip off because he had pleurisy, or inflammation of the lungs. His father feared Peter would get chilled and that would worsen his condition.

The vessel was last seen at Trout River on a Tuesday night, November 30, when a vicious northeast gale reared its head unexpectedly and caused general havoc with shipping along the coast.

Veterans of the sea who last saw *Maria Margarita* believed the schooner was in danger of dragging its anchor on the point near Trout River and apparently put out to sea. It had offloaded its cargo that day and most likely had no ballast, leading to decreased stability in high seas.

By the next day, December 1, no one had seen the vessel and it had not reported anywhere. The first public news of concern for its fate was published on December 11, 1943, in the west coast paper *The Western Star*. It said, "No reports have as yet been verified and great anxiety is felt regarding Captain Dicks and his crew."

Other subsequent reports claim the smashed hull of the schooner was found days later off Lobster Cove Head near Rocky

Harbour. This was miles up the coast from where the schooner had been anchored. Others say one of its dories drove ashore, but no bodies were ever found. There are those who still remember the fateful night *Maria Margarita* was lost and when the wind howls in late November-early December the people who know the story refer to the gale as "like the one the night Captain Dicks and his sons were lost."

Some years later Young's schooner *Miss Glenburnie* left Port Saunders bound south for Humbermouth with lumber for Batten Brothers or W.J. Lundrigans Ltd. Its crew too met a vicious gale, but sailed on, trying to reach their home port of Bonne Bay. No luck; they were caught out in a dangerous storm. They were fully loaded and decided to "heave to" and await an opportunity to head the vessel in a northeast direction and to return Port Saunders.

They apparently spent a very harrowing night, battling the storm and reviving their memories of the fate of the *Maria Margarita*. They felt they had hove to in the vicinity where Skipper Dicks and his crew had lost their lives some years before. The howling winds and lingering memories blended with reality and the supernatural that night for the Youngs saw and experienced the unworldly.

When *Miss Glenburnie* did beat back to Port Saunders, the Youngs said that during the height of the storm, the Dicks' crew came aboard their schooner - up over the side and stood on the decks. No doubt, from the sad and mournful look on their ghastly faces, the lost souls were looking for shelter from the storm.

No doubt Walter Young and his sons, well-respected, industrious and honest citizens that they were, were reluctant to tell such a story once safe in port. These were straight forward men who would not joke of such matters nor fabricate a fanciful tale. They fully believed what they related, although such an apparition was beyond their comprehension. Others, knowing the hard-working Youngs, were sure they had encountered something very unusual out there in the storm.

They remained in Port Saunders for quite some time until absolutely certain weather would permit them to make the full run back to Humbermouth. This was the last time *Miss Glenburnie* visited Port Saunders; shortly after this trip, it was sold to J.B. Patten and Sons at Grand Bank. The Youngs had another schooner, the *Nepsya* which they lost by fire and that, in effect, ended their connections with the sea and the schooner coasting trade.

In its new career on Newfoundland's south coast *Miss Glenburnie* was again involved in the unusual. On May 24, 1955, it left Halifax with a cargo of lumber and general supplies for Grand Bank and Fortune. A few hours out of port, near Egg Island and about 25 miles east of Halifax, it was rammed by a large freighter. Captain Sam Pardy of Harbour Mille had command of *Miss Glenburnie* for that spring.

Miss Glenburnie (above) in later years, the early 1950's. Courtesy Everett Osmond.

The freighter steamed on into the darkness, leaving the sinking schooner behind. Fortunately the partial cargo of lumber helped keep the wooden schooner afloat and Captain Pardy and his crew had a half hour to get ready. They had time to gather personal effects, launch the dory and row away. For seven hours they rowed, finally tying on to a navigational buoy until morning. At daylight Captain John McGuire of *Josephine K* saw the dory, picked up the stranded men and carried them to Whitehead, Nova Scotia. Pardy said after,

> We were on an easterly course with the steamer approaching in the opposite direction in a thick fog. We heard the steamer's whistle sounding at intervals both before and after the collision. I feel the captain of the steamer would have stopped if he had known he had struck another ship.

Captain Pardy estimated the large ship to be between five and six thousand ton. It hit *Miss Glenburnie* on the bow, near the cat head and split the ship in two. It was later believed the culprit was the Saguenay Terminal freighter *Sunprince*. When *Sunprince*, with slight damage to its bow, was investigated in Halifax, nothing could be proven and the ship which put the final blow on the eerie career of *Miss Glenburnie* remains unidentified.

Trapped in the Cabin

Date:	*10,1893*
Location:	*Bay of Expoits*
Fatalities:	*2*
Remarks:	*Two Girls Trapped Below Deck*

R are are the sea stories from Newfoundland where women are lost in shipping calamities; stranger yet are the tales when all men survived and the only persons drowned were women. But this was the case long ago in the Bay of Exploits, an inner bay within Notre Dame Bay. One can only ponder the horror and desperation of two girls trapped in the cabin of a capsized schooner, hoping against hope someone would soon chop a hole in the hull and pull them out.

In October 1893, Clara Manuel and another girl left Laurenceton, Notre Dame Bay, aboard the schooner *Tamarack*, bound for some port further up the bay, possibly Exploits Island or Twillingate.

Tamarack was built at Exploits Island in 1888 by Luke Manuel, listed in the census as a farmer planter of the island. His schooner was 73 feet long, 23 feet wide, 9 feet deep, and was 84 gross ton. In the fall of 1893 it had a load of lumber aboard as it left Laurenceton.

While parts of this account have been passed on through family generations via the oral tradition, the complete story of how two young girls perished and the men survived is not completely fleshed out. But it was a horror of the sea not likely to be quickly erased from family tales. And the story is verified to some degree in a brief paragraph in the October 31, 1893 edition of *The Harbour Grace Standard*.

Apparently shortly after departing Laurenceton, the load of lumber shifted on deck and *Tamarack* capsized. All the men (who were probably on deck working the ship) climbed up on the schooner's side and lived, but the two girls were trapped below in the cabin. They survived for quite a while, but eventually drowned when the schooner sank near the northeast end of Thwart Island, near Point of Bay.

According to the newspaper, *Tamarack* "met a heavy squall of wind near Grego, which threw the schooner on its beam ends" or with sails and masts parallel to the water. Eventually, if not uprighted, schooners in this condition may turn completely over or sink to the bottom. Grego (or High Grego as it is often known) is located about 8 miles north of Point of Bay near Exploits Island. The schooner drifted towards Thwart Island, near Point of Bay, and the next morning local residents recovered the bodies of the girls.

While the identity of one girl has not yet been determined, family tradition says Clara was 18 years old, the daughter of Jacob and Phoebe (Moores) Manuel of Cottrell's Cove, Notre Dame Bay. Her gravestone stands today in the United Church Cemetery in Laurenceton.

Ship statistics show *Tamarack* never sailed again. Perhaps the schooner was totally wrecked or maybe the painful memories of two deaths aboard the vessel were too much and the ship was not refloated. At any rate its official registry closed out in 1894, a few months after the tragedy.

Veteran mariners at Exploits tried to put this single wreck and double loss of life into perspective, pointing out the irony of it all. "That same fall," they said, "when *Tamarack* was lost there were several shipwrecks on the Labrador coast, none with loss of life."

They were right. Three shipwrecked crews were brought to Newfoundland's north coast by the government steamer *Windsor Lake*. The schooner *Verbena*, owned by Mark Osmond of

Morton's Harbour, was wrecked September 18 at Cape Mugford. Dropped off at Exploits Island were Skipper Richard Bonne (or Boone), Solomon Osborne, Joseph Jewer, John Late (Layte), Stephen James and Benjamin Lush. Isaac and Henry Dawe were landed at St. John's. Arthur Hutchings of Adam's Cove near Western Bay lost his schooner *Lily* on September 24 at Jacob's Harbour. His crew - skipper George Hutchings, Arthur Hutchings, H. Hutchings, Joseph Murray, George Martin and Susannah Hollett - were brought to Western Bay, Conception Bay.

John Steer's schooner *Blossom* was wrecked on September 25 at Kelly's Point near Francis Harbour Bight, Labrador. John Ivany, master, and William Curtis were brought to St. John's, Edward Lane to Greenspond and N. Sparkes to Bay de Verde.

Gravestone of Clara Manuel at the United Church Cemetery, Laurenceton. Some family members claim Clara died of exposure awaiting rescue. Newspapers and the stone claim she drowned. Photo courtesy Mae Whorton and Beverley Warford.

Yet, away on the remote coasts of Labrador 20 crew, including one woman cook, in three ships were wrecked in a span of a week and all 20 survived. Then so close to home, Exploits Island, one ship had capsized, snuffing out the lives of two young women.

Fire Aboard a Dynamite-Laden Ship

Date:	*07, 1964*
Location:	*Off Nova Scotia*
Fatalities:	*None*
Remarks:	*Destruction of M.V. "Trepassey"*

M.V. *Trepassey* had a load of explosives aboard. It was the summer of 1964 and gas and oil explorations off Nova Scotia, although in its infancy stages, were in full swing. Shell Canada chartered three ships for the exploratory work: *North Star VI*; *Polar Star*, a Norwegian vessel; and the 137-foot long *Trepassey*, a Newfoundland-built ship that was once part of the "Splinter" fleet.

One day in late June 1964 while off Nova Scotia, the M.V. *Trepassey* lost the packing around its propellor shaft and began taking on water at an alarming rate. Captain Cecil Walters decided to head for shore, hoping to beach the ship before it sank, but incoming water stopped the engines before it got very far. The crew began to ditch cargo to lighten *Trepassey* enough for the pumps to be effective. The *Polar Star*, upon reaching *Trepassey*, put a motor launch over the side and managed to get a gas-powered pump aboard the sinking ship. This was successful in stemming the inflow of water and *Trepassey* limped into Halifax for repairs.

M.V. Trepassey in Halifax below the MacDonald Bridge. As a result of a 1942 Board of Trade recommendation that ships be constructed in Newfoundland with Newfoundland materials, ten identical wooden vessels were built at Clarenville between 1944 and 1947 for the Department of Natural Resources.

Designed by William J. Roue with the construction supervised by Reuben Carpenter of Little Catalina, they were named for Newfoundland settlements: Bonne Bay, Burin, Clarenville, Codroy, Exploits, Ferryland, Glenwood, Placentia, Trepassey and Twillingate. Termed "double-enders", with the stem and stern similar, they were to be used as minesweepers and cargo ships. Locally these "Clarenville" vessels became known as the Splinter Fleet. Note the crow's nest for spotting seals on the foremast.

For the loss of Splinter Fleet vessel *Bonne Bay*, see Chapter 11 in Volume Two. Photo courtesy Hubert Hall, SHIPSEARCH Marine

Cape Breton Post

YEAR NO. 170.   SYDNEY, NOVA SCOTIA, SATURDAY, JULY 18, 1964   24 PAGES   PRICE 10 CENTS

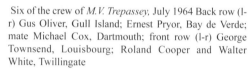

Dynamite-Laden Ship Explodes, Crew Is Safe

Oil Explorations Delayed By Blast

Six of the crew of *M.V. Trepassey*, July 1964 Back row (l-r) Gus Oliver, Gull Island; Ernest Pryor, Bay de Verde; mate Michael Cox, Dartmouth; front row (l-r) George Townsend, Louisbourg; Roland Cooper and Walter White, Twillingate

By mid-July it was back on site about 75 miles south of the Halifax lightship. As part of the oil exploration group, *Trepassey* and *Polar Star* laid the explosive charges along the seismic line and were termed "shooting" ships. *North Star VI* was the instrument ship, recording the seismic waves.

A typical load of explosives aboard a shooting ship was 250 ton of a nitrate-based explosive and the charges required a cap and booster to ignite. About 200 ton was stored aboard *Trepassey* along with caps and boosters. At this time the vessel had eight crew and six oil exploration scientists or engineers aboard.

About 6 p.m. on July 16, someone saw a fire near a generator in the engine room. While the crew tried to put out the blaze with extinguishers, it was difficult to get at the source of the fire in the partitions. Soon the power failed. *Trepassey* now had no SOS by radio and was unable to signal the other ships with lights. One of the engineers, Mark Craig, used a battery powered loudspeaker

Crew of *Trepassey* July 16, 1964

Captain Cecil Walters, LaHave, NS
First Officer Michael Cox, Dartmouth, NS
George Townsend, Louisbourg, NS
Gus Oliver, Gull Island,Conception Bay, NL
Ernest Pryor, Bay de Verde, NL
Roland Cooper, Twillingate, NL
Walter White, Twillingate, NL

to alert the other two ships, working less than a mile from *Trepassey*.

Not long after Walters called for all to "abandon ship" and soon they were picked up by *North Star VI*. *North Star VI* and *Polar Star* remained close. To warn other ships they positioned themselves over two miles away on each side of the burning *Trepassey*.

One of the surveying engineers, Craig Condon of Halifax, was aboard *Polar Star* and remembered that:

A passenger liner emerged from the light fog and refused to reply to repeated calls by the captain of *Polar Star*. However, when he sent a message say-

ing that there were three ships to the liner's starboard and that the one in the middle was on fire with 200 tons of explosive on board, the liner still failed to respond, but left at full speed!

North Star VI, came over to the burning *M.V. Trepassey* and rescued its crew and workers. Photo courtesy Hubert Hall, SHIPSEARCH Marine

A couple of hours later, around 8 p.m., smoke was seen to emerge from *Trepassey*. At that point the other two ships moved away to a distance of two and a half miles on either side. Flames were seen later, but the explosive charges needed caps and boosters to cause them to explode. The caps and boosters were stored in a container on the forward deck.

The *Polar Star*, the third vessel engaged in exploratory work off Sable Island in July 1964. Photo courtesy Hubert Hall, SHIPSEARCH Marine

That deck finally burned through just after midnight and *Trepassey* exploded.

The shockwave from the explosion was felt quite violently on the other ships at a distance of 2.5 miles. Captain Walters, in a ship-to-shore message to Halifax, said: Everyone aboard *Trepassey* rushed around with fire extinguishers, but we got choked up with smoke. So we put out the boats and rowed away from the vessel.

Once in the lifeboats and into a contrary wind, the eight crew and six geophysical surveying engineers had to row hard to keep the boats from drifting into the ship.

Safe aboard the other vessels, *Trepassey*'s crew watched their burning ship until 12:30, Friday morning when it went up with a tremendous roar and a heavy blast. Walters recalled: "The whole sky flared like daylight. You could see pieces of debris and wreckage flying all over.

At daylight, the other ships sailed through the last location of M.V. *Trepassey*. Small pieces of wood were all that remained. That day the Coast Guard vessel *Raleigh* picked up the crew and landed them at Lunenburg.

Ole Nielson, managing director of the Trepassey Shipping Company of Dartmouth which had the ship chartered to the Shell Oil Company, said *Trepassey* was valued at $100,000 and had much valuable geophysical equipment on board.

Fortunately none of the fourteen men aboard had any injuries. After they were landed, Captain Walters went to Lunenburg where he resided, Chief Officer Cox, a retired Halifax harbor pilot, went to his home in Dartmouth. The others looked for transportation to their homes in Newfoundland or Nova Scotia. As a

Stamp commemorating *Trepassey*'s work inthe South Atlantic. Photo courtesy Hubert Hall, SHIPSEARCH Marine.

footnote of personal marine tragedy, Mark Craig, the engineer who summoned help from the burning *Trepassey*, was later lost at sea from *North Star VI* while working off Sable Island.

Trepassey's long and varied career was over. Chartered by the Royal Navy in 1946-47, it made two trips to the Antarctic under Captain Eugene Burden of Carbonear. The second trip - the British Grahamland Expedition - provided weather reports for the Falklands and its dependencies. On returning to St. John's, it engaged in the fish-carrying trade with Captain Harry Thomasen of Grand Bank in command. In 1950 it was purchased by the Windsor Trading Company, and chartered by CNR for the northern Labrador service. Later, Captain Harry Stone took *Trepassey* to the Arctic. As an icebreaker in the 1950s, it assisted Bowater's paper-carrier ships in the Bay of Islands.

Sold in 1962 to maritime shipping interests, it often carried dangerous goods. In the summer of 1963 it transported a load of explosives from the St. Lawrence River to the Dutch Islands of Curacao.

The Half Man of Trinity Bay

Date:	*10,1915*
Location:	*Off Belle Isle*
Fatalities:	*None*
Remarks:	*Herbert Johnson Saves His Ship "Oriental"*

Herbert Johnson, barely 14 years old, of Trinity Bay landed in New York in November of 1915. He claimed he was a half a man, but that half was enough to save a full ship from shipwreck - a statement some reporter with the newspaper *New York Sun* found amusing and different. The tale was so unique young Herb's story was published in the New York paper.

Johnson's mother and three younger sisters were already living in United States, but he stayed in home in Trinity Bay to earn some cash. When he has his stash of cash pocketed in November, he joined the Red Cross liner *Stephano* in St. John's and went to New York. He had his summer's savings, $153, in his pocket for his mother. After the father drowned, Herb's mother and sisters had migrated to Bridgesport, Connecticut, and to reach Bridgesport Herb traveled on the regular steamer line from Newfoundland to New York. And there he told his story.

Herb, barely into his teens, was a breadwinner. His father was lost at sea off Trinity Bay two years previously and Herb became the sole support of his mother and sisters. The *Sun* said he was, at 14 years old, already "a hardy sailor of the Northern seas, a sturdy youngster, tall for his age and weather beaten from his work at sea." He had first gone to sea at age twelve, the summer his father was lost, as a cabin boy and general helper.

A typical Newfoundland schooner picks its way gingerly through pan ice, bergy bits and growlers. The men on deck keep a close watch.

When interviewed for his amazing story of saving a ship in distress, he wore a little green cap and walked with a deep sea roll of a veteran sea dog.

But Herb smiled with his winsome face and red cheeks as he spun a yarn.

> There were nine men and a half on our ship this summer, not counting the lady cook, and the half a man was me. They shipped me on at half share to cut cod throats and help haul traps when needed. I was fairly new at the fishing and not old enough to get a full share. The girl cook was my cousin Martle Gable, 19 years old and as a neat a hand at

cooking as one would wish to see." (The girl's name could be a pronunciation misunderstanding by the American reporter and may be the Newfoundland name, Myrtle Gabriel).

In July 1915 Captain Peter Randell of Port Rexton, Trinity Bay, asked Herb to work with him on his 78-ton schooner *Oriental*. Randell fished off Belle Isle in the Straits, about 300 miles from Trinity Bay. The grounds that summer were prolific as they often were and the crew did well. But come late October, Herb Johnson had earned more than his half share and he modestly told a tale of his real worth to the newspaper:

About three weeks ago (end of October, 1915) Captain Randell and the eight whole men put off in the dories to haul the cod traps, leaving the half of a man - me - and the girl to look after the boat. All of a sudden we got caught in one of large ice floes that often come down through the straits. The ice pack carried away our anchor and chain and started sweeping the *Oriental* toward the rocky shore. I piped all hands on deck, which of course was only my cousin Martie and ordered her to take the wheel. I then raised the jumbo, the big jib, while Martie steered. I raised the jumbo easy; I could haul it up with one hand.
Meanwhile the ice had piled up over the decks, carried away a lot of the deck gear and taken some of the cod back overboard. We were now being carried straight for the shore. A bit of fresh wind sprung up and we squeezed out of ice pack and make for Lark Tickle Cove on Belle Isle - one of only two harbors on the large island with safe anchorage and shelter.
Here we got another anchor from a schooner lying there and put out to sea again to pick up the men in the dories. They had been scattered by the ice, but

we managed to find them all. Martie was as good a seaman as the best of them.

We made a record catch for the *Oriental* this season, 900 quintals of cod.

With that Herbert Johnson finished his story. "Every word of it true," he said of the half man who, with the help of a girl cook, saved the schooner *Oriental*. The newspaper man had a twinkle in his eye for the lad, so confident, but yet so modest with his Newfoundland yarn.

objcctive of the Austro-German and Bulgarian armies now invading Serbia is the capture of this railroad. Note the mountainous country of Serbia.

FISH EXPORTS TO GREECE PROHIBITED

Following is a copy of a letter received by E. A. Payn, Secretary of the Board of Trade and posted at the Trade Rooms yesterday.

Nov. 10th. 1915.

Sir,—

I have the honour to acquaint you that His Excellency the Governor-in-Council has been pleased to issue a proclamation, following the terms of that issued by the Imperial Government, whereby exportation of fish of

NEWFOUNDLAND BOY SAVED SHIP AMID ARCTIC FLOES

He and His Girl Cousin Got Nine Men to Safety.

A hardy sailor of the Northern seas, barely 14 years old, who with the help of a girl saved a schooner caught in an ice floe from going on the rocks and rescued the nine men of the crew

brador.

Total catch brought home—3400 qtls.
Total Shore catch, (traps and boats) —250 qtls.
Total from all sources to Nov. 1st— 3650 qtls.
The Notre Dame, Jno. Hackett, master, was lost at Sloop Hr., Labrador with 500 qtls.

GERMANS ON SHORT RATIONS

London, Nov. 4.—Entirely upon the evidence of their own latest official publications, it is manifested that the Germans' food situation on the threshold of the second winter of the war is much more serious than in November, 1914.

DON'T L

NOT to give al

St.

We Beef. M

Author's After Word

There was a time when harbours around Newfoundland and Labrador were seemingly full of sailing ships; a forest of masts and spars. In the nineteen twenties proud citizens could boast, "In the spring just before the fishing season began, sure you could walk across our harbour stepping from one schooner to another." Yet within twenty years the era of the schooner and steamer, as a chief mode of transportation, passed and the harbours lay empty.

The sea was and, to a certain extent, still is a dangerous calling. As the mariners in their ships sailed away, stories of shipwrecks and fire at sea, tales of abandoning schooners in fierce Atlantic storms and litany of missing ships became more numerous than ever. Added to the ever-present natural hazards there were, in the 1930s and 1940s, new elements of risk for schooners - the rum smuggling trade, the threat of attack by German subs in World War Two and frequent collisions with large ocean liners steaming across the fishing grounds.

Good Reader, that's the way it was - danger and mystery in an era of sail in which our hardy mariners and island pioneers worked hard and sacrificed much. Then, by the 1960s, the sailing ship and the coastal steamer faded from existence. It became, to paraphrase Margaret Mitchell, a time that in the twinkling of an eye was "gone with the wind."

Often the era when men stood before the mast is viewed nostalgically, but it was not always a glorious and happy period. So many vessels and lives were lost that the effect it had on disrupted and devastated families must have been tremendous. And personal stories of hardship and grief were compounded with the economic setbacks that wrecked and missing ships had on communities large and small.

That, in essence, is why I chose to commemorate *Salt Water Tales: The Strange and Tragic, Illustrated* to a woman, a bronze woman. She's a statue, a monument, a Mariners' Memorial, representing the strength and determination of women all over Newfoundland and Labrador. She also represents mothers and wives who lost husbands, brothers, sons, fathers to the sea and she's going to stand, looking out to sea, in my hometown of Grand Bank. I also will donate a percentage of the sales of this book to help fund this tremendous venture of erecting the Memorial in the year 2007.

Due to the large number of sea adventures and misadventures as of yet unrecorded i.e. new tales of harrowing events, the stories will be continued in word and image in Volume Two of *Salt Water Tales: The Strange and Tragic, Illustrated*.

Robert C. Parsons
October 2004

About the Author

Robert "Bob" Parsons has been called one of the most popular and prolific writers on the subject of Atlantic Canada's ships and ship disasters. He is the author of fourteen non-fiction books, ranging from *Lost at Sea, a Compilation* and *Toll of the Sea* to *Wind and Wave* and *Born Down by the Water*. His work has also appeared in a number of newspapers and magazines such as *Downhomer*, *The (Evening)Telegram*, *Newfoundland Quarterly* and *Newfoundland Lifestyles*. A former fish plant worker and educator and a present-day researcher and devotee of all items marine related, he lives in Grand Bank, Newfoundland.

The author has made every effort to properly identify, credit and obtain publication rights for text and photos in this book. If there are any errors, omissions or oversights, notify Robert and corrections will be made in any subsequent reprints.

About the Illustrator

Mel D'Souza is a self-taught artist who was born in East Africa and went to school in his native Goa - a former Portuguese territory in India. In 1971, he emigrated to Canada with his wife and two daughters and settled in Brampton, Ontario. They spent their summer vacations travelling extensively by road across Canada and the United States, before 'discovering' Newfoundland in 1989. Since then, Mel has returned every year to visit as much of Newfoundland and Labrador as possible and, more recently, bought himself his 'second home' in Francois on the South-west Coast.

Sources

CHAPTER 1
Year of the Great Storm *The Evening Telegram* November 7, 1921
Arctic and **Vesta** *Public Ledger* October 3, 1854
Early Tragedy of Herring Neck Personal information from Phyllis Rendell
Steiner, Salt Harbour, Newfoundland/New York; written information from
Albert Warren, grandson of William Warren, Herring Neck; *Morning
Chronicle* April 19, 1877
Bickley *The Evening Telegram* "Offbeat History" March 11, 1985; Personal
correspondence with Gordon P. Williams, Westbank, BC, whose great great
aunt perished on the ship; excerpt from Captain Bob Bartlett's book *The Log
of Captain Bob Bartlett;* **Hibernia** Correspondence from Joan Carrigan,
descendant of Captain James Stapleton
Dove *The Patroit* May 26 and June 19, 1871; **Atlantic** *Montreal Gazette*
June 4, 1840
United Brothers and Captain Paul Hall *Western Star* April 3 and 17,
1901; March 26, 1902 and June 24, 1903; Correspondence with the great
granddaughter of Captain Hall, Peggy (Gale) Bennett, formerly of
Stephenville
Victory *Harbour Grace Standard* December 13 and 27, 1895
Susan *Evening Mercury* March 28 and 29, 1887

CHAPTER 2
Brothers *Evening Mercury* October 24, 1887; correspondence with Thomas
Cole
Admiral Drake *The Daily News* November 28 and 29, 1927
Customer Murphy, James. *Newfoundland Heroes of the Sea.* 1923; *The
Royal Gazette* September 5, 1843
"Carbonear Island" Unidentified newspaper clipping; Personal conversation
with Lloyd Rossiter, Carbonear
Magnolia *Evening Herald* December 3, 1894
Rose of Sharon Two unidentified and undated newspaper clippings; **Jenny**
The Twillingate Sun October 26, 1883
Freddie Walter *The Halifax Herald* May 10, 1895
Canima Personal information from Lee Harper, grandson of one of the
Harpers shipwrecked on *Canima*; Personal information from Bride Martin
and the people of Peter's River who helped me find out more about Gull
Island; *The Morning Herald* Halifax, September 7 and 25, 1883; *The New*

York Times September 7 and 8, 1883

CHAPTER 3

Valliant *The Daily News* April 29, 1897; *Evening Herald* April 29 and May 3, 1897

Electra (schooner) From an article taken from *The Chronicle*, May, 1909

Kitchener *The Daily Times* October 20, 1931; *The Evening Telegram* October 20, 1931

Trixie H *Evening Mercury* May 23, 1887; **John Knox** *Evening Mercury* May 5, 1887

Florence Personal correspondence from Charlene Gill, Alton, Ill., and the late Dorothy Kavanagh, Hartford, Conn.; *New Era* September 3, 1840, and information taken from Robert Parsons' *Raging Winds...Roaring Sea*, Creative Publishers, 2000

River Dale *Western Star* October 21, 1936

Poppy *The Evening Herald* October 5, 1893

CHAPTER 4

Essex Unidentified newspaper clipping

M.F.B. *The Halifax Herald* April 9, 1920; *The Evening Telegram* April 19, 1920

Nellie Dixon *Sydney Post Record* May 27, 1946; **Green Rock** *The Halifax Herald* July 16, 1953; *Harbour Breton Coaster* "Culture Corner" March 5, 1992; personal conversation with Aloysius Baker, Harbour Breton

South Head *The Evening Mail* (Halifax) December 6, 1926; an account of Helen Mathers (South Head) supplied by George Walters, Fortune; **W.C. Smith** *Halifax Evening Mail* December 6, 1926

A.D. Storey *Halifax Herald*, June 28th, 1895

Fortuna *The Harbour Grace Standard* January 31, 1896; Thomas, Gordon. *Fast and Able.* Gloucester 350th Celebrations, Inc., 1973

Potomac Various editions of *The Western Star* from February 11 to the end of March, 1914

C.A. Roland Personal correspondence from Tammy MacLeod, daughter of shipowner Chessel Irving; personal conversation with Philip Power, Louisbourg, NS, formerly of English Harbour West, NL; correspondence from William Chapman, North Sydney, NS; *The Guardian* Charlottetown, PEI, May 22, 1962

Saxilby *The Daily News* November 16, 17 and 18, 1933; personal correspondence from Christine ?

CHAPTER 5

John *The Fisherman's Advocate* May 10, 1929; **Mary** *Ledger* November 17, 1868; **Edward** Personal information from William Maguire, Groton, MA, descendant of Thomas McGrath and James Flynn; Jerome Walsh, Marystown; *Observer's Weekly* December 13, 1938

Six Brothers Correspondence with William Pellerin, Exeter, New Hampshire; eclark@syd.eastlink.ca; gravestone inscriptions

Lady May and **Clio** *The Evening Herald* undated article; *The Daily News* January 28, 1896; personal correspondence from Judy (Moores) Patey, ?, New Brunswick; special help from Lloyd Rossiter, Carbonear

Grover Cleveland *The Harbour Grace Standard* April 20 and May 20, 1892

Speedwell Personal conversation with Eric Day and Betty Brenton; poem "The Sailor's Grave" from *The Morning Chronicle* February 2, 1848

Sigrid *The Evening Telegram* December 7, 1903; *The Daily News* December 11, 1903; *The Western Star* February 13?, 1905; Monument inscriptions at Ferryland; special help from Maxine Dunne, Ferryland

General Horne *The Evening Telegram* December 17 and 26, 1920; an account of **General Horne** supplied by George Walters, Fortune; personal correspondence from Marion Collins, Barrie, Ontario (grand-daughter of Captain Berkley Rogers); personal correspondence from A. Ross Pomeroy, a descendant of the LeDrew's of Change Island; personal conversation with the late Clarence Griffin, Grand Bank who knew the connection between *Marion Belle Wolfe* and *General Horne; The Book of Newfoundland Volume IV*. Ed. Joseph R. Smallwood, 1967, page 84

Pendragon *The Daily News* July 31 and August 1, 1914; *Twillingate Sun* October 17, 1914 and another October 1914 *Twillingate Sun* clipping; Calvin Evans *For the Love of a Woman* Harry Cuff Publications, 1992

Arabella *The Royal Gazette* January 15, 1881

CHAPTER 6

Coquette and **"The Funks"** Correspondence from Howard Rohloff, North Haven, CT; *Royal Gazette* April 6, 1852; *Evening Mercury* October 8, 1888

Wally G Various editions of Nova Scotian papers; *The Evening Telegram* July 24, 1978; **Catherine M** *Halifax Herald* October 22, 1931

William Inman *Book of Newfoundland Volume III*. Joseph R. Smallwood, Editor. Newfoundland Book Publishers, p. 458-460; *The Morning Chronicle* December 13, 1870; folk history of the Gallops through whom by intermar-

riage with my g g grandfather, Aaron Forsey, the author is distantly related
Fleetway Personal conversation with William Taylor of Millertown and son Gordon Taylor, Halifax/Truro; **Dominion** Personal correspondence from Bruce Hynes, Eastport

Miss Glenburnie Written correspondence from Michael Caines, St. John's; *The Evening Telegram* May 26, 1955; *Halifax Chronicle-Herald* May 27, 1955; and *The Family Fireside* June, 1955; **Maria Margarita** Personal conversation with Peter Dicks, the son of Captain Dicks, in Corner Brook; *The Western Star* December 11, 1943; photos and information from Everett Osmond, Woody Point

Tamarack Correspondence with Beverley Warford, Fortune Harbour/Point Lemington, and George White; *The Harbour Grace Standard* October 31, 1893

Trepassey Personal conversation and correspondence from Craig Condon, Halifax; *Cape Breton Post* July 18, 1964; *The Chronicle Herald* Halifax, July 18 and 20, 1964

Oriental "Herb Johnson's Story" Several people in the Trinity Bay area helped find information on the persons (Captain Peter Randell and Herbert Johnson) featured in this story including: Josephine Johnson and Clarence Dewling, Trouty, Millie Johnson, Port Union and Fred Rex of Port Rexton; *The Daily News* (through *The New York Sun*) November 12, 1915

Index A
(Volume One)
Ships, Towns and Landmarks

Index B

People and Businesses